THE TRIATHLETE'S GUIDE TO

D0617775

Swim
Training

THE ULTRAFIT MULTISPORT TRAINING SERIES

Going Long: Training for Ironman-Distance Triathlons, Joe Friel
and Gordon Byrn

The Triathlete's Guide to Bike Training, Lynda Wallenfels

The Triathlete's Guide to Off-Season Training, Karen Buxton

The Triathlete's Guide to Run Training, Ken Mierke

The Triathlete's Guide to Swim Training, Steve Tarpinian

Available Fall 2005:

The Triathlete's Guide to Half-Ironman Training, Tom Rogers

The Triathlete's Guide to Mental Training, Jim Taylor, Ph.D.

Available Spring 2006:

The Duathlete's Guide to Training and Racing, Eric Schwartz

The Triathlete's Guide to Sprint Distance Training, Gary Bredehoft

THE ULTRAFIT **VELO** MULTISPORT TRAINING SERIES *press*

THE TRIATHLETE'S GUIDE TO

Swim Training

Steve Tarpinian

VELO press

Boulder, Colorado

The Triathlete's Guide to Swim Training
© 2005 Steve Tarpinian

Before embarking on any strenuous exercise program, including the training described in this book, everyone, particularly anyone with a known heart or blood-pressure problem, should be examined by a physician.

Printed in the United States of America.
10 9 8 7 6 5 4 3 2

Distributed in the United States and Canada by Publishers Group West.

Library of Congress Cataloging-in-Publication Data

Tarpinian, Steve
   The Triathlete's guide to swim training / Steve Tarpinian.
         p. cm.
   Includes index
   ISBN 1-931382-57-3 (paperback : alk. paper)
         1. Triathlon—Training. 2. Swimming—Training. I. Title.
   GV1060.73.T37 2004
   796.42'57—dc22

2004023551

VeloPress®
1830 North 55th Street
Boulder, Colorado 80301–2700 USA
303/440-0601 • Fax 303/444-6788 • E-mail velopress@insideinc.com

To purchase additional copies of this book or other VeloPress® books, call 800/234-8356 or visit us on the Web at velopress.com.

Cover by Erin Johnson, EJ Design; Cover photo by Don Karle
Composition by Dianne Nelson, Shadow Canyon Graphics
Illustrations by Andrea Varalli

To the memory of my grandmothers:
Irina Russo and Heripsime Tarpinian

Contents

Foreword ix
Preface xi
Acknowledgments xiii

1 Why Swim? 1
2 Freestyle Swimming Techniques: The Basics 11
3 Freestyle Drills: Technique Training 33
4 The Off Strokes 53
5 Advanced Freestyle Techniques 67
6 Pool Training 85
7 Open-Water Swimming 105
8 Dry-Land Training for Swimmers 117
9 The Finishing Touches 129

Appendix A: Defining Your Goals 135
Appendix B: Training Programs 139
   8-week Sprint Competition/Speed Work   140
   12-week Sprint/Olympic Triathlon   143
   16-week Long-Distance Triathlon   148

Appendix C: Additional Resources 155

Flexibility Training   155

References   156

Additional Reading   157

Publications   157

Swimming Organizations   158

Index 161

About the Author 171

Foreword

I've known Steve Tarpinian for 8 years, but I've known him through his writing for nearly 15 years. When I began looking for someone to write a book on swimming for the Ultrafit Multisport Training Series, Steve was an obvious choice. Not only is he well-known in the sport, but he is also a master swim technician who has been learning about and teaching swimming for most of his life. As a teacher, he has had students from raw beginners to seasoned professionals. His previous books on swimming have proven to be treasure troves of knowledge.

If you are new to the sport or looking for that last elusive 1 percent that will put you on the top step of the podium, you will find this book to be an excellent resource. Steve's carefully crafted strategy for building and refining your swim technique is described here in such a way that athletes at all levels can relate.

The emphasis of this book is on the freestyle technique because that is the most common stroke for fitness swimmers and triathletes. Learning and refining the freestyle is no small task. The movement patterns are quite complex when compared with other sports such as cycling and running. Although it's certainly important to improve your fitness for triathlon swims, the key for most triathletes is to improve their efficiency in the water. This is Steve's mission in writing this book. Here he takes you through the intricacies of the freestyle stroke along with drills to enhance your technique.

Steve Tarpinian is a master teacher. Follow his carefully planned guidance described here, and I am confident that you will soon find yourself effortlessly swimming faster.

JOE FRIEL
ULTRAFIT MULTISPORT TRAINING SERIES EDITOR

Preface

I would like you to answer the following question: Does the world need another book on swimming? My desire is that your answer is a resounding yes, especially after you've read this book! Having already written two successful books on swimming, I realized that I have learned so much about swimming, in terms of both technique and training, from the athletes I have worked with that a new book would add additional insights to every athlete's enjoyment of swimming, whether for triathlons, swim competition, or simply fitness. One of the main elements of this book is not so much in innovation of new techniques (happily, our basic concepts from previous works hold up really well) but rather in new ways of getting us to implement better technique and better training.

This book will cover what all swimmers need to know for creating an improvement program for their technique and training. In addition, a proven plan for taking up the challenge of open-water swimming, for both competition and training, will be explored.

Although I wrote the book to be read cover to cover and refer to prior chapters often for reminders on technique and training, an athlete may jump around to any chapter of interest. All athletes will do well to read Chapter 1 to get a good basis for the ideas presented as well as some interesting swimming facts to share at dinner parties! So, dive in, enjoy, and I hope we can share a lane soon!

Acknowledgments

When I left my job as an electrical engineer 20 years ago to become a swim and triathlon coach, I (and others) thought I was crazy. Not only did I leave a lucrative career, but I also dove into a field that did not yet exist. The main reason why I made the change was that I realized my desire to be around athletes and help them reach their goals. I did not know that these same athletes would help me reach mine. This book and any of my other creations in the field of coaching would not be possible without all the athletes whom I have had the good fortune to coach. I wish I could have another volume to list all your names, but you know who you are. Thanks!

Special appreciation goes to Jean Mellano who, in addition to being the woman in my life, is also my best friend. Next, I want to acknowledge all my fellow teammates from around the globe on Team Total Training. Your excitement of swimming and triathlons at every conceivable level, from first-timer to world champion, inspires me daily. I have been on some amazing teams in my athletic career, but the energy on this team is something truly special. Thank you.

My powerful inner circle of support comes from Jean Mellano, Marianna and Richard Tarpinian, Marian Zahra, Helen Cane, Steve Muzzonigro, Peter Perkins, Frank Smith, Randy Weintraub, Adolph and Anna Gasper, Josephine Picinic, Doug Thralls, Paul Thomas, Alex and Maria Terrazas, Mike and Jackie Barth, Joe Collins, Jason Rivas,

Andrea Varalli, Valentina Rudokas, Wataru Shimizu, Robert Shorin, Chris Pfund, and Andreas Lindberg.

My assistant coaches: Annette Gasper, Mike Trunkes, Cyle Sage, and Craig Longobardi. We learn together.

Thanks to Joe Friel for his invitation to have this book be a part of his series.

Last, my good friend Rip Esselstyn, who has generously shared many of his feelings about swimming with me in numerous discussions about technique and training, has helped me understand what I teach. More than anything, I have enjoyed our yearly pilgrimage to the Coast Guard buoy in Kailua Bay.

CHAPTER

1 Why Swim?

The main goal of this book is to create your own best stroke and training. This book gives you the tools you need to improve your swimming. Upon finishing this book, you can expect to have a proven plan to improve your swimming. Then all you need to do is follow it.

Over 20 years ago, I started working with athletes to improve their swimming, but my coaching philosophy was developed 10 years earlier. When I was 12 years old, I started swimming year-round. I was below average for my swim club, but I was an above-average baseball player. At 14, I felt I needed to choose between being a competitive swimmer and a baseball player. It was a hard decision, made worse by the fact that my swim coach suggested I stay with baseball! When I finally made up my mind, I realized I was choosing swimming for the challenge of it and my love for the sport. I was out to be the best I could be.

My main focus was freestyle mostly because it was the fastest stroke and that excited me. My approach was to learn everything I could about technique and training. What I quickly realized was that my idols (including Mark Spitz) at the time were not all swimming with exactly the same technique. That was the key: to find my own perfect stroke. That is what you must do, too. I and other coaches will offer the framework, but I propose to you that anyone who says that he or she has the exact and only recipe for swimming is off base (no pun intended, regarding baseball).

My technique philosophy is simple: Learn how to relax and breathe in the aquatic environment, and use basic physics and some cutting-edge techniques to create an effective individual stroke. Reinforce the physics and new techniques with lessons from studying the fastest swimmers in the world.

WITH LIMITED TIME TO TRAIN, WHY SPEND IT SWIMMING?

If you feel like you get a better workout in 30 minutes of running than swimming for the same length of time, you would be partially correct. Running is more taxing on your body than swimming because of gravity. In addition, you do not have the water to cool you when running, so your body has to work harder to cool itself down. Or maybe you are a triathlete and believe that because swimming is a small portion of the triathlon, training on the bike will pay bigger dividends. True; however, "the beauty is in the balance," and you must consider and realize these overwhelming facts:

- Swimming is a lifetime activity.
- Swimming can save your life.
- You need to be able to swim to participate in all water-related sports.
- Swim technique is challenging, hence rewarding.
- Swimming is a great recovery for all other sports and life's stresses.
- Swimming efficiently not only will make you faster in the swim but can leave you with more energy to perform better in the bike and run in a triathlon.

We have established that it is worth our time to swim, so the important question is, How long should we swim?

HOW MUCH TIME IS WORTHWHILE?

The answer is three to six times per week, three being the minimum to provide you with some carryover benefit and the reinforcement effect for your technique work. More than three sessions is for the athlete who is looking either to improve rapidly or to reach a very high level of fitness. Another exciting thing about swimming is that these sessions can be as short as 20 to 30 minutes and still be an effective training session for both technique and fitness.

In sports like running, more is not necessarily better, but in swimming, usually more is better. How many sessions per week and how long they should be are dependent on the following factors:

- How much time do you have available? Let's face it, you may want to swim for 2 hours, but if you have only 45 minutes, then it is what it is. Make sure your training sessions match your lifestyle and schedule, or you will be frustrated.
- Are you new to technique training? It may be challenging to make technique changes. It requires a great deal of focus and visualization. For this reason, shorter sessions with more frequency are the most beneficial.
- What are your goals? If you have an Ironman triathlon race in 2 months, you'd better schedule a 60- to 90-minute swim workout at least once per week. On the other end of the spectrum, 30 to 45 minutes would suffice if you are training to stay fit or prepare for the local sprint triathlon.
- What level of competition and fitness do you desire? Is competition for you about simply improving fitness? Or are you out to see what your absolute potential is? These are two very different reasons for swimming and will obviously require different amounts of time and energy.

Chapter 6 will take you through the nuts and bolts of training.

IS SWIMMING AGELESS?

What are the main variables for improvement in an aerobic sport?

- **Technique.** Technique entails how you use your body to apply forces and reduce resistance. This is the technical aspect of training.
- **Training.** This is the workout, where the intensity is the focus, not the technical aspects of the activity.

- **Recovery.** Recovery involves many areas that allow the body to regenerate—eating, sleeping, getting a massage, doing easy exercise, meditating, reading, stretching, laughing, and just plain relaxing.
- **Psychology.** Many coaches believe that this area holds the greatest potential for an athlete. Sport psychology involves techniques such as visualization, positive thinking, and acknowledging and releasing blocks.
- **Nutrition.** Bad habits have a way of creeping up on us. The basics are pretty irrefutable: Hydrate, eat whole foods, and customize your diet with the foods and percentages of macronutrients that suit you best.

The techniques in running and biking certainly have their complexities, but compared with swimming, they are relatively simple. While this distinction may create some frustration for the swimmer, it also contains a large potential for improvement. This is what allows swimmers to improve in spite of the aging process.

Have you ever been to a masters swim competition? Something happens at national and world masters swimming that does not happen in running or cycling: 40-, 50-, and 60-year-old athletes setting personal records! Many of these swimmers were competitive when they were in their 20s; some were even Olympians. How is this possible? Are they stronger? More flexible? No, they are using different techniques and training methods. In spite of being less powerful and flexible than in their youth, they are swimming faster! That is pretty exciting—who does not want to look forward to an improvement curve that can last a lifetime?

Recently during a swim workshop, an athlete asked me, "Do you ever get tired of doing these swim seminars?" I gave that some honest thought and responded, "No, I never get tired because there are so many technical aspects of swimming to work on that I am always challenged to find the best approach for each swimmer to help him or her improve."

An exciting aspect of swimming is that it is a lifelong sport. Every athlete I know enjoys the lifestyle of being an athlete and staying fit. Hopefully all of us will live healthily and happily into our 80s, 90s, or beyond. While the pounding from running and the possibility of a crash and a broken hip from cycling seem too risky at those ages, swimming remains the perfect activity for athletes of every age.

The challenge, the goal: Find your own unique "perfect" stroke. Hopefully this perspective will have you rushing down to the pool to do some technique drills to work on getting more streamlined and more powerful. Before you run off to the pool, be sure to have a plan for improvement (Chapter 3 gives you this plan).

IN PRAISE OF SWIMMING

I find triathletes' perspectives on swimming fascinating. A significant number of triathletes view swimming as a "necessary evil," an event to get over with (as fast as possible) so they can get on with the triathlon. A similar attitude is common among fitness swimmers: They love the feeling they get from swimming, but the actual activity of swimming they see as a means to an end. While evolution has helped foster these feelings due to biking and running being land activities and us being land mammals, consider another perspective that I hope will empower you to higher levels of enjoyment and performance: The challenge and journey of working and seeing your swimming improve is itself a rewarding activity.

Two of the most common goals listed on the data sheet at our triathlon camps are "to remain active and healthy as long as I can" and "to improve as much as I can for as long as I can." Out of the three disciplines in triathlon, swimming offers the most opportunities for these types of goals.

Without question, the number one activity prescribed by health advocates and doctors alike is swimming (and other water activities). The reasons are numerous, most surrounding the fact that swimming is a no-impact sport that has few injuries and can be done in spite of many physical conditions (minor and severe). You would think that with this fact, swimming would be hands down the number one exercise in terms of participation. It is rated pretty high, but certainly not number one. Why? Swimming is not an activity that everyone knows how to do (as is walking or jogging); it is a learned skill in an unfamiliar environment, it is not required for survival, and the technique involved is challenging.

If you are not proficient at something, your enjoyment is diminished. The better you are at swimming and the more you see your speed and efficiency improving, the more you will enjoy and do it. But first there is something holding all of us back (some more than others).

THE CHALLENGE: WHAT HOLDS US BACK?

We are land animals. Okay, so this may not be the most earth-shattering news you have ever heard. However, this fact is one of the reasons swimming is such a difficult skill to master. Depending on your beliefs about evolution, humans may have "walked" out of the water at some point in his development (did you know human embryos have gills?), but in 2005 and for many years before then, humans have been land animals.

Why is this fact so important? Most people experience a tension that is either subtle or very apparent when they are in the water. This tension in many ways is a survival instinct. It keeps us alive. Without question, swimming can be a life-or-death activity. As soon as your head goes under the water and you are no longer able to breathe, the natural reaction is to hold your breath and try like heck to get your head out of the water to breathe again. Makes sense, but the problem is that you send your entire mind and body into the "fight or flight" mode, which makes swimming efficiently virtually impossible.

Analyzing many beginning swimmers, we realize this phenomenon is quite obvious. We see them literally jerking their head up out of the water with every stroke to get a breath, usually accompanied by short, fast arm pulls mostly pushing the arms down to keep the head up. In other swimmers, the signs may be subtler, but the effect on the swimmers' efficiency can still be very significant. It then becomes a vicious cycle that is reinforced every time you swim unless a change is made. Unconsciously, this is the conversation the brain is having with the muscles: "Push arms down to keep the head up to breathe and see"; "I have to push down, and again I am sinking"; repeat. . . .

The results of this knee-jerk reaction of being uncomfortable in the water, with your arms pressing down to lift your head to breathe, are as follows:

1. **Breathing is short:** Reduced oxygen intake occurs due to holding of breath and the body going into fight-or-flight mode.
2. **Legs sink:** As a person lifts her upper body vertically, the lower body must go down. This increases the drag (resistance) created since the area of the body creating resistance is increased tremendously.
3. **Pull is short:** This reaction happens because the feeling a person gets is "If I stop pulling, I will sink"—and this is correct because the body position and direction of the pull are causing the vicious cycle described earlier.

These results lead to lots of energy expended with a poor return in terms of distance swum.

The good news is that along with being land mammals, we have a large capacity to think, reason, and experiment to develop better ways of surviving. Once the body can get out of this survival mode, a whole new world opens up: the endless road of improving efficiency and speed.

To fully appreciate this point, we need a little history.

A BRIEF HISTORY LESSON

It is amazing how much freestyle swimming has improved in the last 100 years. Virtually every improvement has come from a swimmer trying something different and getting faster. It is generally accepted that all swimming strokes developed out of some form of breaststroke, which makes sense, because breaststroke is the easiest stroke during which to breathe and see where you are going. Drawings unearthed in the Middle East and dated back to 9,000 B.C. depict people swimming something resembling the breaststroke. Breaststroke training was also a standard part of both ancient Greek and Roman military training.

Many credit the American Indian with first doing a "crawl," having the arms recover (move from the end of the pull back to the beginning of the pull) over the water. In addition to this looking like a crab "crawling" through the water, swimming speed increased significantly because of the following factors:

- Longer pull: The pull could be longer, providing more propulsion (effective power).
- Elimination of arm recovery resistance: The resistance of the recovery was eliminated. All that extra resistance from recovering the arm under the water was eliminated due to the arm recovering over the water.

One of the most significant improvements came when swimmers started putting their head in the water and rolling to the side to breathe, as opposed to keeping the head up and out of the water. The head-in-the-water position allowed a swimmer not only to have a better streamlined position (since the legs were not forced down as much) but also to take longer strokes (longer extension is possible when rotation of body occurs). This change of putting the face in the water is usually credited to the Australians (for many years, people have referred to modern freestyle as the Australian crawl). I have heard the story that this major development in swimming happened because the Australians needed a way to get away from the crocodiles. Of course, being the practical jokers that Aussies are, one can picture an Australian coach tossing in a crock after sending his swimmers off for a 25-meter sprint!

The instinct to push down and lift the head is basically a fear of drowning. It is also often unconscious. I love the way that many motivators teach people to face a fear, especially this one:

FEAR = False Evidence Appearing Real

Fears can be good and bad. They can save our lives, but they can also keep us from reaching our goals and potential. Defining and recognizing what the fear is all about are essential.

Fear of Water Defined

Fear of the water is what holds many athletes back from maximizing their enjoyment (not to mention performance) of swimming. It is important first to assess which type of fear you have before you can effectively work on it. We have found that there are basically two categories of fear that swimmers can have:

- Fear based on a bad experience (usually from childhood). Let's call this *core fear.*

- Fear based on the fact that a swimmer's skill and/or confidence is low, and the possibility of tiring, struggling, swallowing water, and even potentially drowning is real. In plain talk, such a swimmer really cannot swim. Let's call this *skill fear.*

The situation gets sticky when you have a mixture of the two, or worse, when a person has core fear and mistakes it for skill fear. This creates the all-too-common phenomenon of a swimmer who tries everything and just cannot seem to get any better or more comfortable. Until core fear is faced and reconciled, improving swimming is an uphill battle.

Core fear is something that is best handled by getting in touch with the experience(s) that caused that fear. We have had very good results when we have athletes describe the experience and acknowledge the scariness of the experience and then realize that it is in the past and does not need to control current feelings and reactions. If it is very traumatic and deep-seated, a consultation with a psychiatrist or psychologist to work on freeing that block may be helpful. Avoid being embarrassed—everyone has challenges to overcome, and acknowledging something like this is the first step in accepting it and moving on. This realization can and should be a very powerful experience.

Skill fear is much more straightforward to work on. As long as you have some good coaching and guidance, you can improve your skills as a swimmer. A snowball effect happens as you improve and become more confident. So the important thing is to get started down the road to improvement. What is the best way to do it?

First Things First: Relax

One of the biggest problems we see at our clinics is that swimmers, who have no problem swimming a thousand or more meters, are still swimming as though it was their first time in the water: showing lots of tension, holding breath, and using their arms to push water down instead of back. All swimmers can benefit by learning to relax in the water and be comfortable with the fact that although swimming can be dangerous, you need not be in survival mode every time you swim. Although most swimmers know this intellectually, they fail to translate it to their physiology. Perhaps it is

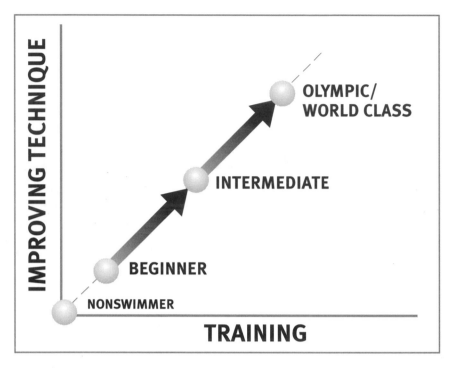

1.1 Swim Improvement Curve

time to take a deep breath and acknowledge that you may not be ready for Olympic trials, but you can swim pretty well and can start to relax in the water. This will allow you to make some changes in your technique and squeeze a little (or a lot) of efficiency out of your technique. (For any reader who literally cannot swim, there is no shame in that, and starting with a basic beginning swim class at your local YMCA or community college is the best start point.)

Figure 1.1 is what I call the swim improvement graph. Your goal should be simply to move up the curve, not see how fast you move or where others are in relation to you on the curve. These thoughts and concerns will only distract you and slow your progress. Basing your success on others' skills and performances is a poor way to gauge your progress. Working on moving up this curve is a rewarding and lifelong process. Let's begin!

CHAPTER

2 Freestyle Swimming Techniques:

THE BASICS

WHY FOCUS ON FREESTYLE?

Freestyle is exactly that: freestyle, any style you choose. Because the crawl is the fastest style, it has become synonymous with freestyle. To be the fastest, it must be the most efficient and powerful. For this reason most fitness swimmers and triathletes swim freestyle. Even in swimming competitions, more events and relays are swum in freestyle than in any other stroke. In addition, many facets of freestyle carry over to learning the other strokes. For all these reasons, it is the best stroke to master first.

This does not mean you should ignore the other three major swimming strokes. We will cover these in depth in Chapter 4, because they are very important in helping you develop your feel for the water and in balancing your muscle development. Sometimes it is even advantageous to start a beginner with another stroke first to help him relax. Let's take a deeper look at this notion of relaxing in the aquatic environment.

Relax and Learn to Tread Water

Most of the challenges of relaxing in the water are related to very real and normal instinctual responses, as we learned in Chapter 1. In most cases, overcoming these responses is the biggest obstacle to getting on the path to swimming in general and then to maximizing one's skills and ability. If you have not already addressed this matter, please review Chapter 1 to see what is underneath any tension or nervousness you may have about swimming or simply being in the water.

"Tread water—what? Why would I want to spend time practicing staying in one place? I want to move, cover distance . . . " I know, but having the confidence that you can tread water easily will help you relax. When you know that you can "stand" in the water, there is less urgency in each stroke. Think about running. When you go out running, you have no fear of walking or stopping if you get a cramp, feel sick, or just plain need a break. That is because you know you can stop and walk without even thinking about it. Treading water is like stopping to walk or stand while running. Knowing that no matter what may happen, you can stop and easily stay in one place to relax, rest, or regroup is very powerful. You can breathe freely, look around, and stay calm.

In addition to helping you relax and be more comfortable in the water, knowing how to tread water—and efficiently to boot—is important for other compelling reasons. An example is that some triathlons have deep-water starts with 1,500 to 3,000 swimmers. Waiting in water over your head at the start of such an event for 10 to 15 minutes is necessary. You'd best do it with as little energy expended as possible!

It amazes me how many relatively proficient swimmers look at me like I have two heads when I ask them to tread water. They never were taught this skill, and when they learn it, they are amazed at how much more relaxed they become.

What to Do

To tread water efficiently, move your hands in a sculling (side-to-side) motion with the hands pitched (angled) in as they come toward each other and pitched out as you move them away.

Depending on your buoyancy (women float better than men) and the water's salinity (floating is easier in saltwater), a kick may or may not be needed to tread water easily. If the hand movement is not enough, a gentle kick will provide the added lift you need. This kick can be a nice, gentle alternating forward-and-back motion of the legs while lying slightly back.

Figure 2.1 illustrates the motion of the arms while treading water. Note that the angle of the hands faces out when you move the arm/hand out and in when the arm/hand moves in. This angle is slight, about 20 degrees.

Recommendation: Five minutes of treading water once a week. Once treading water is comfortable and natural, practicing it is unnecessary.

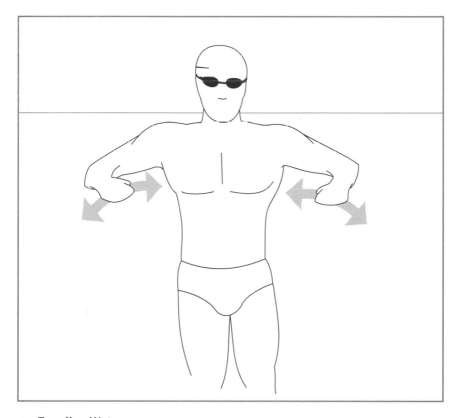

2.1 Treading Water

I was conducting an open-water session at Kailua Bay in Kona, Hawaii, for a group of 20 athletes preparing for the Ironman® world championship in 1996. I was briefing them on our agenda for the swim session. Their first task was to warm up to the first buoy about 200 meters out and meet me there. Off we went. When I got to the buoy, I noticed one of the athletes, Jennifer, was swimming circles around us. I joked with the other athletes that she must have been a shark in a prior life. I finally grabbed her and held her up while I treaded water and asked her why she was not stopping. She looked at all of us dumbfounded and said, "If I stop swimming, I'll sink!" This remark made me realize not everyone knows how to tread water. It also made me realize that the logical fear of sinking is serious: drowning.

As I looked around I realized that all the participants in the session were struggling a bit and nodding in compassion for Jennifer's plight. These were among the best triathletes in the world. Not necessarily swim specialists, but they were all capable of swimming 2.4 miles under a cutoff time. It dawned on me that many of them had learned how to swim and never had learned how to tread water. I do not think I would have the courage to swim without the skill to tread water: What if my goggles come off? What if I get a cramp? What if I swallow water?

I restarted that session with a little instruction on treading water, which made everyone relax. We were then able to make a lot more progress when we started to work on the other elements of open-water swimming. I was amazed that I never had made this realization in my 10-plus years of coaching this group of athletes. From then on, treading water has been a standard part of our first session with swimmers.

BREATHING

Before we even start talking about swimming technique, we need to take a good look at breathing. There are two parts to explore: the transfer of oxygen into the body and the actual mechanics of breathing. My experience shows that swimmers at every level can improve their breathing.

Transfer of Oxygen

Oxygen is a key ingredient in the energy production cycle and is ultimately needed to sustain life. One of the most important things in swimming freestyle is to breathe out while your face is in the water so that when you roll to the side, you get a full inhalation of air. Because of being tense in the water, however, many beginning swimmers hold their breath completely; then when they roll to the side, they must breathe out before they can breathe in. What happens to these swimmers (and most swimmers do this to some degree) is that they get less air in than they otherwise could since the time that the mouth is out of the water is used up expelling air. Invariably these swimmers need to breathe every stroke and usually get winded after a short swim, not from the effort but merely from lack of oxygen. This becomes a vicious cycle of never really getting a full breath in but rushing for another.

Elite runners have taught me the importance of breathing in swimming. I have had several sub-2:30 marathoners seek my coaching to help them swim better for crosstraining and possible triathlon racing. The first time I worked with one of these athletes, Paul, I watched him swim a length, and although he had some technique errors to correct, he swam pretty well. But, as he warned me, he was completely out of breath after one length. He was upset because he felt that with his superior cardiovascular fitness, he should be able to do at least a few laps without stopping. Confused, I agreed.

I asked Paul to swim again and looked to see whether he was breathing. I saw that, in fact, he was breathing every two strokes. I decided to take a look from under the water. What I saw was Paul holding his breath, not blowing out. Now I took another look over the water and realized that although he was turning his head to the side, he was not breathing, in or out. Problem solved: Of course he could only do one length—he was completely out of oxygen! He did not even realize he was not breathing. He thought his performance was because he was a thin runner with a poor swimming technique.

We did some breathing exercises at the side of the pool, and within a half hour he was swimming 20 lengths straight. This story may be an extreme example, but it is not uncommon. Even accomplished swimmers can make the transfer of oxygen more smooth and efficient.

What to Do

Always focus on breathing while warming up and cooling down. This is the perfect time to smooth out your breathing and relax in preparation for the technique work and main set (actual workout) to follow.

One of the most frequently asked questions from swimmers is, How many strokes should I take between breaths? There is no simple answer. Individual physiology prevents coaches from being able to give cookbook solutions to most training questions and challenges. Experience, however, can help us give accurate guidelines to help athletes.

Breathing Patterns

In distance freestyle swimming, you should take breaths at the time that is appropriate for you. Some swimmers take a breath every two strokes (sometimes referred to as every stroke because you breathe every time you stroke on one side, but it is actually every two strokes). Fewer breathe every third (also known as bilateral breathing, since every third has you alternating sides). Fewer still breathe every fourth or fifth stroke. The two variables that determine how often you need to breathe are lung volume and swimming intensity.

Lung Volume

Just as some athletes have large hearts and lower heart rates due to the increased blood volume pumped with each contraction of the heart, if an athlete has a larger lung, the volume of air inhaled is greater, and hence more oxygen is transferred to the blood with each inhalation; in other words, there is more oxygen. More oxygen means the athlete can take more strokes after each breath.

Recommendation: Next time you are warming up for a swim workout, notice whether you are exhaling and how smoothly you exhale between breaths. You need to find a good rhythm for your breathing. Fine-tuning your breathing pattern is much harder in swimming than in other aerobic sports since you must time it right or you end up with a breath full of water.

This technique is one of the most important first steps in swimming efficiently; for many swimmers, it is even more important than any stroke technique improvements, since without oxygen, well, you know what happens: no air, no life. Most top professional athletes, just like their amateur counterparts, breathe every stroke.

Working with professional triathlete Jurgen Zack, I was surprised to see him breathe every fourth or fifth stroke, but he felt that if he breathed earlier, he had not used up his oxygen. The logical conclusion is that his lung volume must be larger than most other swimmers'. This example highlights the need to individualize your technique.

Swimming Intensity

It makes sense that the harder your effort is, the more oxygen you use. While your stroke rate goes up as your intensity and speed increase, it does not increase quite as fast as oxygen consumption. (At least it should not: The less efficient your stroke, the faster your stroke rate will increase, but that is a discussion on technique, not breathing.) The important point to understand here is that for easy swimming, you may have no trouble breathing every third (bilateral) or even every fourth or fifth stroke, but when you really start to crank, you need to breathe every two or three strokes to fulfill your oxygen requirements.

Recommendation: Do a set of four to six 100-meter swims; alternate between fast and slow for the entire 100. Take 15 seconds' rest after each swim. Experiment with different breathing patterns to see what works best.

Alternate or Bilateral Breathing

Almost every swimmer I have ever worked with (including myself) has a preferred side to breathe on. The rotation of your body will always be better on that side, because you rotate more on that side to breathe. It is important, however, to be comfortable breathing on both sides. What this really means is comfort rolling or rotating to both sides. This rotation technique is at the core (pun intended) of efficient swimming. We call this the *long-axis rotation* of freestyle because it is best visualized by an imaginary axis through the spine that your body rotates around.

It behooves you to develop the skill of bilateral breathing for the following reasons:

- It balances out your stroke, by rotating equally to both sides.
- It allows you to see things on both sides (obviously important in open water).
- If the timing for your breathing is best at three strokes, you will be able to swim with this breathing pattern and maximize your oxygen utilization.

What to Do

All drills that work on rotation (i.e., drills 1 to 5 in Chapter 3) are helpful in developing a balanced rotation. Make rotational drills a part of every practice.

What breathing pattern should you use? It depends on your intensity, your lung volume, and how well you transfer air in and out. Some swimmers need four or five strokes to utilize all the oxygen that one full breath provides them; others start to go into oxygen debt after three strokes. How do you find out what is best for you?

Recommendation:

2 × 100-meter freestyle swims with 30 seconds' rest as follows:
Length 1: Breathe every two strokes.
Length 2: Breathe every three strokes.
Length 3: Breathe every four strokes
Length 4: Breathe every four strokes.

Do this drill once a week, and you will find the best breathing pattern for you. Also be sure to breathe out fully while your face is in the water so that when you roll to breathe, you can spend all that time breathing in.

Breathing exercises at the side of the pool are essential for all beginners and anyone struggling with breathing. Look at Figure 2.2 to see the breathing practice at the wall of the pool. Standing in the shallow end of the pool, bend at the waist while holding on to the wall or gutter with one hand. Put the other hand behind your back and place your face in the water; now practice blowing out with face down and roll your upper body to the side to breathe in.

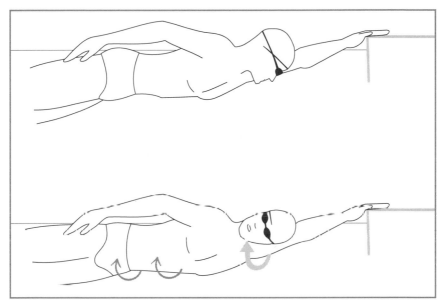

2.2 Poolside Breathing Exercises

Recommendation: Do five on each side. A good way to do this exercise is to do a round of breathing (five breaths on each side) followed by a 50-meter swim; repeat five times.

When you can tread water and breathe properly, you are well on your way to becoming an efficient swimmer. Next, you can work on the mechanics of a good body position and pull. Working on stroke techniques before mastering breathing and relaxing is putting the cart before the horse.

SWIMMING PHYSICS 101: UNDERSTAND AND APPLY BASIC PHYSICS TO SWIMMING

You do not need a background in physics to understand two important physics principles that apply to swimming faster and more efficiently:

- Reduce drag (improve body position).
- Increase power (propulsion).

Do not be confused by the fact that I listed "reduce drag" first; it does not mean that this principle is more important than increasing power. Reducing drag can be translated to having a streamlined body position. Body position in the water is a function of many things, including speed. The slower you move, the more you sink.

The idea that great swimming is all about body position has become a major source of confusion and frustration for swimmers in the last 15 years. There has been an overzealous focus on body position, to the point of neglecting any work on providing powerful propulsion. About 35 years ago, swimmers were encouraged to swim "flat" (no rotation) and have a very high stroke rate (number of strokes or pulls taken each minute). As coaches started to notice that the fastest swimmers in the world were rotating, it became clear that the human form is much more streamlined when on its side and as parallel to the surface as possible. With this awareness, a revolution was started that looked more and more at all the benefits of body position.

Some schools of thought hold that if the body position is correct, propulsion takes care of itself. The better your streamlined form or body position, the faster and farther you will go with the same forces applied. Obviously this point is important; however, no matter how good your body position is, with no power you go nowhere. The logical conclusion is to improve both as best you can and become the best swimmer possible.

Synergistic swimming is what happens when the benefits of both improved streamlining and increased propulsion are present and create an effect better than either alone.

As you can see in Figure 2.3, the first swimmer is using his arms to push water down, which has two bad results for swimming: It creates a body position that has a lot of drag, and most of the resultant forces are down, not back. Keeping in mind Newton's law of forces acting in opposite directions, we need to push water back to move ourselves forward (this is a very simplified summary of the forces in swimming; Chapter 5 explores the details). Almost all swimmers, even some really good swimmers, do this to some degree because it is a natural response. Remember, lifting the head up to breathe and see is an instinct, so don't get down on yourself

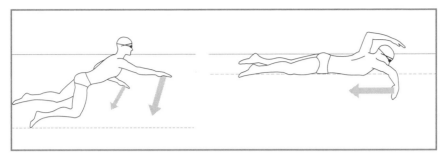

2.3 The Physics of Swimming

for this habit; simply acknowledge it and relax to improve. The swimmer on the right applies his forces back and rolls to the side to breathe. Both these actions help maintain a great body position in addition to maximizing the propulsive forces.

Take another look at Figure 2.3. This illustration reveals the importance of rotating your entire body about an imaginary axis that goes through the spine and down to your feet and up out the middle of the top of your head. You should breathe by rotating to the side rather than lifting your head. This eliminates the need to press down with the arms. When you no longer need to press down with your arms, you can work on bending the elbow at the beginning of the stroke to pull back.

Rotation and breathing are very much integrated. Figure 2.4 shows this long-axis rotation looking at the front of the swimmer.

When rotation is efficient and smooth, efficient breathing (the mechanics of having your head laid out on the side pressing on your shoulder and your mouth above the water) is a natural consequence. When you are not taking a breath, your head is stationary. Figure 2.5 shows the body on the side integrated with breathing position.

Freestyle Kick: The Flutter

Few people understand the importance of the kick in freestyle swimming for distance and fitness. This is understandable for the following two reasons: (1) Many swimmers are such poor kickers that their kick actually creates more drag than propulsion. Logically, if you swim faster with less effort (no kicking), why kick? (2) Other

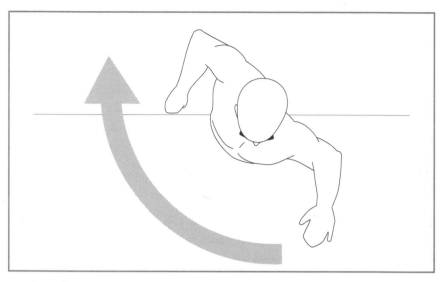

2.4 Rotation

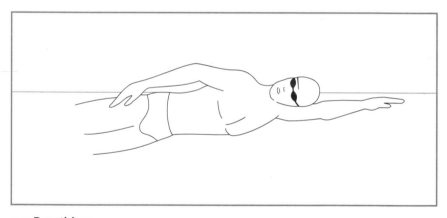

2.5 Breathing

than during sprints (swims of 100 meters or less), the kick does not offer any appreciable propulsion.

What many athletes incorrectly assume is that kicking is a waste of energy. The fact is that an efficient, easy kick is at the foundation of a good body position. If the kick is used properly, it helps get the body in optimum streamlined position to take full advantage of every pull. We are not talking about a powerful kick, but an *efficient* kick that helps keep the legs up (reducing drag) and helps rotate the body in alignment. When a swimmer drags her lower body from side

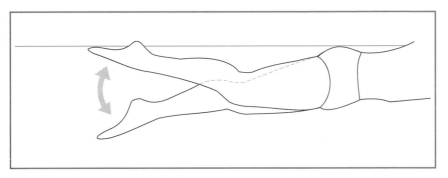

2.6 Flutter Kick

to side (called *fishtailing*), she is creating unnecessary drag. Driving the rotation from the kick and core helps keep the body aligned and long. Therefore, the key is in a small kick that stays in the slipstream (a narrow band of area that has minimal exposure out of an imaginary "hole" made in the water as your body moves) and is coordinated with the pull and rotation.

The kick in freestyle is called a *flutter kick* because the legs alternate in opposition, "fluttering," while keeping the legs "long," meaning that the feet are pointed and the knees bend only slightly at the end of the leg movement. The most common mistake in flutter kick is bending the knees too much. This creates too much drag since it comes out of your slipstream. When the legs come too far out of this slipstream, the added resistance slows the body down more than the kick's power provides speed.

Another very important factor in the efficiency of the kick is the ankle range of motion. The better an athlete can point the toes, the more potential he has as a swimmer. In fact, many college coaches require a threshold minimum angle of flexibility or they will not accept a swimmer into their program because they believe it is a limiting factor of the swimmer's potential. Some gains can be made by stretching the muscles in front of the shinbone (e.g., the anterior tibialis).

Notice that in Figure 2.6, the toes are pointed and the knee is hardly bent. Imagine a tube around the body with just enough room for this kick. This tube would be the streamline of the kick.

Freestyle Arm Cycle

Although many discussions of swimming technique start with what the arms do when pulling, I like to focus on this part last, because by the time we discuss the arms, the foundation is in place to take full advantage of the additional power that they generate. The drill sequence in the next chapter will reinforce this priority by teaching you the rotation and body drills first before the arm cycle, or what are commonly referred to as *pulling drills.*

The pull in freestyle is your "engine." A great kick can provide propulsion, but it uses much more energy and hence can only be used for short periods of time. In distance swimming, the kick is responsible for 0 to 5 percent of the propulsion depending on the swimmer's skill and effort of kicking. That leaves 95 to 100 percent of the propulsion to come from the pull.

The five phases of the arm cycle are listed here. A *stroke* usually refers to one complete arm cycle. During phases 2 and 3, there is an in-and-out sweeping of the pull that adds power to your pull. It is very important to note that for learning how to swim efficient freestyle, you should try to allow this motion to come as a natural consequence of long-axis rotation as opposed to actually adjusting the arm pull. In effect, it is best to visualize pulling straight back and let the body rotation make a natural sculling motion. The following five phases of the pull will allow you to get the most efficient power to provide your body with propulsion.

The Five Phases of the Arm Cycle in Freestyle

Entry. Enter the hand in the water and extend the arm forward. Your goal is to do this as smoothly as possible. Ideally the hand should enter 20 to 30 centimeters (8 to 12 inches) in front of the shoulder. This means the angle of entry is about 45 degrees and your elbow is bent a little. Use your long-axis rotation to help extend the arm forward just under the surface of the water. Ideally your hand should enter thumb first, and as you extend the arm forward, the whole arm rotates toward your center (medially), and at full extension the palm is parallel to the bottom of the pool (or ocean, lake, etc.).

Elbow bend. This phase is sometimes called the *catch* because you are in a sense "catching or gripping" the water to prepare for the power phase. This elbow bend is important so that you have a large pulling surface. In addition, the elbow bend enables you to use the powerful muscles of your back to provide more power to the pull phase. Without good and early (as far forward as possible) elbow bend, the pull will be less than optimal.

Pull. Phase 3 is the power phase. The pull is the actual movement that propels you forward. As your arm passes the shoulder, you start to straighten out the elbow and use your triceps to finish the pull.

Release. A slight outward rotation of the arm frees the shoulder to prepare for a relaxed arm recovery.

Recovery. Bring the arm back from the finish of the pull to the entry to start the arm cycle again. Ideally the arm should be very relaxed and have a slight bend in the elbow so that the hand is not higher than the elbow. As the hand passes your head, it should be slightly facing you to protect your shoulder.

Figure 2.7 shows the five phases of the pull.

THE PUSH-OFF

Although technically not part of freestyle, the push-off from the wall while swimming in a pool is important for all strokes. Every time you push off the wall, you have an opportunity to improve your streamlined position. A good push off allows you to start each length with a little speed and a good body position (see Figure 2.8).

Take a glide off the wall, then kick about 6 to 10 kicks (keeping your arms together in a streamlined position) and start stroking. The key is to time it properly: Do not start swimming immediately upon your feet leaving the wall. You should take a glide off the wall and then have a good strong kick *before* starting your pull. If you start kicking and pulling too soon or too late, you will slow yourself down from the speed that a good streamlined push-off provides.

Is a streamlined push-off in a sense cheating? There are no walls in the open water to push off or do a flip-turn on. Answer: No, it is not cheating; as a matter of fact, it is one of the best things that you

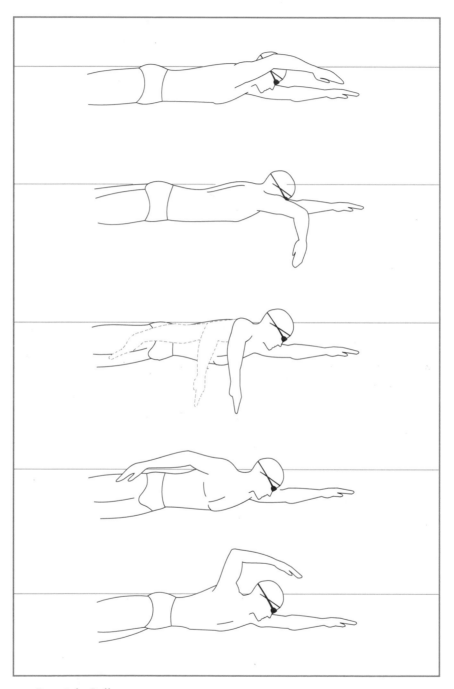

2.7 Freestyle Pull

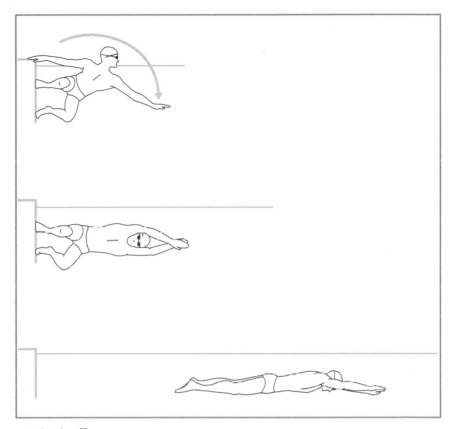

2.8 Push-off

can do to get faster. To become faster, you need to feel and know what "faster" is. Due to the propulsion of the legs pushing off the wall and the reduced drag of a streamlined form, it is virtually impossible to swim any faster than the speed of a good push-off. It is like getting a little taste of faster swimming at every turn, which is really good.

In addition, if you do what many fitness and triathlete swimmers do and hardly push off at the wall because you think you get a better workout, think twice. Yes, there are no walls in open water, but there is also no stopping every 25 meters and starting with little to no speed. What happens then is that you spend the entire length of the pool increasing speed only to stop and start again. So use the walls—they are a boost that helps you learn good body position and swim faster overall.

LEARN FROM THE BEST

Although we all need to find our own individual perfect stroke, there is much to learn from the key movements that *every* great swimmer does. This is the approach that I focused on as a young swimmer to make huge gains in my own improvement. As I implemented these key elements, my swimming improved dramatically. In addition, I learned from watching many different forms moving through the water, such as boats and dolphins. Although they were not directly applicable to human aquatic propulsion and streamlining, I learned many lessons that translate in a dynamic and enlightening way. These lessons all match the physics explained earlier.

Olympic Lessons

Ian Thorpe (a.k.a. The Thorpedo) and Grant Hackett (or, as my assistant Annette calls him, Granty) are two terrific swimmers to analyze. What can triathletes and swimmers learn from watching them compete in the 400-meter (Thorpe) and 1,500-meter (Hackett) freestyle races at the Sydney and Athens Olympic Games? Lots—they swam the two longest swimming events in competition, and they won the gold medals. Yes, they have great genetics: Thorpe, for example, has size 17 feet! We cannot change our genetics, but we can change and improve our technique, which is the lesson that these guys can reinforce.

From the surface, we saw how these athletes (especially Hackett) rotate their entire body to get increased power and improved streamline position. Power gets a little boost from the fact that when the rotation is coordinated with the pull, power from your core is added to the pull power. The reduced drag (improved streamline) comes from the fact that the frontal area is reduced since one shoulder is out of the water.

From underwater, we see how well they bend the elbow in the beginning of the pull (as opposed to "dropping" the elbow and pushing the arm down). This motion provides maximum power with each pull.

The moral of the story is not new but is worth repeating: Work on long-axis rotation and early elbow bend in the beginning of your pull to maximize improvement.

Ironman® Hawaii Lessons

Each year my coaching staff and I do an informal study of the swimmers' technique at the Ironman® Hawaii by conducting daily swims in Kailua Bay with hundreds of the world's best triathletes for an entire week leading up to the race. We usually take mask and snorkel and sometimes a monofin so that we can go underwater and swim along the swimmers to study them. Fellow coach and local Hawaiian swimmer Dietrich Lawrence said it best: "They are all loose rafts." That remark was an interesting way to describe what I typically call malaligned or disjointed swimming. Dietrich had just been to a swim clinic with a few of the sport's leading technicians, and that was a term they used. Imagine that you are going surfing. Would you rather paddle on a stiff fiberglass board or a flimsy raft? The obvious answer is a rigid board. You lose way too much energy if the vessel gives as you apply power and attempt to be streamlined.

Watching on race day, I noticed that all the swimmers who swam under an hour were pretty "rigid surfboards," and the rest were "loose rafts." What was the difference? Posture and body coordination. Yes, Mom was right. Good posture is important. Good posture utilizes your core muscles to keep your spine alignment and your back muscles to keep your shoulders and head from slouching forward. Dietrich Lawrence knows this because he sees firsthand what practicing Pilates (which strengthens core muscles) can do for a swimmer. Remember the inside look at a day in the life of Dara Torres during the Olympic trials in 2000? At 3:00 P.M. was Pilates. Dietrich brought the concept of Pilates as integral training for swimmers to Stanford University coaches 10 years ago. I do not know whether you all need to run out and enroll in a Pilates class or session, and I think yoga and other methods of training can also help, but first and foremost be aware of your posture—both when swimming and when on land.

Another observation we made was that triathletes in general have poor posture. I guess hours and hours bent over a bike is not the best thing you can do for your posture. Other exercises, such as back bends and core strengthening, are thus essential for the triathlete who wants to maintain and improve his posture to become a better swimmer.

Boat Lessons

What do a boat and a human swimmer have in common? A lot, in terms of maximizing speed and efficiency.

Generally, the longer and narrower the hull design, the faster the boat can go due to decreased drag. That is why we see the ultimate position for our body is on our side with an arm extended forward, making the body long and narrow. If we had a large fin (like a dolphin), we would stay in that position and just kick to achieve good speed and efficiency. Because we do not, we have to learn how to use our arms for power and leave the slipstream as little as possible.

When we look at boats starting from a zero-speed state, we see that there is a period of time that the boat needs to "plane off," since the stern (rear of the boat) is always heavier than the bow (front of the boat). This action is very pronounced in a speedboat, in which the engine is in or toward the back, and at rest the boat sits very deep. This situation is not too different from a human since our legs are denser than our upper body, which contains the lungs and has less muscle mass.

These lessons are helpful real-world reminders of the importance of the elbow bend in the beginning of the pull, proper rotation and body position, and speed maintenance.

PRACTICE OFTEN

I bet you were hoping this book would give you the magic bullet to improve your swimming. No such luck. Few things in life that are rewarding are easy, and swim improvement is no different. What we are after with the technique drills you will learn in the next chapter is positive, consistent change. We need to change the neuromuscular firing order of our muscles. This is no easy task and is not something that happens overnight or without thought. Practice often. In addition to building and maintaining your aerobic fitness as you would with any aerobic activity, swimming requires more technique work and repetition.

Here is a very common question asked of swim coaches: How often do I need to do technique work? My answer: You need to work on your technique each practice. The best swimmers in the world do—shouldn't you?

INDIVIDUALIZE TO FIT YOUR PHYSIOLOGY

As you become comfortable doing the drills properly, you will start to get a better feel for the water and find your own personal rhythm. Your technique may differ slightly from some fictitious "perfect" stroke, yet it will work better for you.

Janet Evans is one of swimming's most successful distance freestylers of all time. She still holds a world record that is over 12 years old. Janet swam with a windmill recovery (her elbow had no bend in it on the recovery, so it resembled a "windmill")—textbook wrong! However, she used that technique to set multiple world records. That style suited her. Would she have swum faster with a high elbow recovery? We do not know, but I doubt it. Somehow her elbow technique worked for her.

One of the main reasons a windmill recovery is thought of as bad technique is that in most cases, the straight arm recovery is followed by a straight arm pull. The straight arm pull, as described before, adds to poor body position and does not offer optimal power.

It is important to note that in spite of her windmill recovery over the water, under the water Janet did have an incredible pull with a very early elbow bend. I cannot overestimate the importance of bending the elbow at the beginning of the pull in swimming (all the strokes). If you learn and implement only one thing from this book, learn how to be great at an early elbow bend. This technique is one of those key principles that the best swimmers utilize and slower swimmers do not. Find your own perfect stroke.

With this point in mind, let's learn the freestyle technique drills that reinforce these irrefutable basics of great freestyle swimming.

CHAPTER

3

Freestyle Drills:

TECHNIQUE TRAINING

I n this chapter, specific technique drills to reinforce the basic physics of freestyle swimming are described and illustrated. Guidelines for doing the technique portion of your workout are explained. We need some tools to work on this project of creating your own unique and "perfect" stroke. Technique drills are the tools we use to "drill" into our bodies a more efficient way to swim.

Tools are just that—tools. Using a saw, no matter how good the saw is, will not help much in driving a nail into a piece of wood. Not only do we need the right tool for the right job, but we also need to use the tool properly. You can have the best hammer in the world, but if you hold the wrong end, you will not get good results.

ENTROPY: WHAT IS THAT?

Entropy is the measure of the degradation of the universe. We work against entropy in almost every part of living. Swimming is no exception.

It is a law that entropy naturally increases. Ever notice how your desk or car naturally gets cluttered unless you regularly take the time to reorganize and clean it up? Do nothing to make your stroke better, and it will naturally deteriorate over time. Almost every swimmer intellectually knows the importance of working on swimming technique. Many have an idea of how to perform effective drills properly. A few actually practice them. Very few, however, practice them accurately and consistently. These are the swimmers who make dramatic improvements in their swimming. Will you be one of them?

I challenged myself to see how many drills for freestyle swimming I could come up with. I started making up weird ones at about 40 drills. I noticed that many of the drills worked on the same flaws. Next I distilled the 40 drills down to a top 10 list, and I am confident that performing these drills every swim training session will improve your freestyle swimming. This list is by no means exhaustive, and a few more will be explained in Chapter 5. My experience shows that it is much better to have a swimmer master a few drills than do many drills incorrectly.

To get the most from this list, purge all you know of drills from your mind. Do them as though for the first time, and be bold: Make changes in doing these drills. More than likely you will feel a little awkward at first. This awkwardness is a sign you are doing something different and hopefully better. An example is that when a swimmer does one of our kicking-on-the-side drills correctly for the first time, she usually gets water up her nose. Although this sensation is uncomfortable, it is a sign she is doing it right and needs to develop a slight outward nasal pressure to keep the water out. Of course, having a coach on deck who is skilled in making sure that you are doing the drills correctly is the ultimate practice scenario. This is what our swim workouts and clinics are all about.

Terry Kerrigan is a professional triathlete whom I worked with. We had some nice improvement in his swimming speed, solely by focusing on his drill work; he did the same or less volume (distance). One of the interesting things that Terry shared with me was that he knew he was doing the drills wrong when they felt too easy. What he meant was, when he was not doing something different in the drills than he does in his regular swimming, it felt normal. What an intuitive athlete!

We all need to become our own intuitive athlete. At first, changing your technique will most likely feel awkward, which is good. It is a sign you are doing something different. Different does not always mean better, however; seeing yourself on videotape and experiencing improved speed and efficiency are the best verifications of positive change.

USING VIDEO

Another helpful tool for working on your technique is video. Video is useful in two ways:

- Getting yourself videotaped gives you feedback on how you are really swimming and performing drills, as opposed to how you think you look. These two are usually very different, and seeing it for yourself is essential. Video should also be used as a source of feedback to see whether you are truly making the desired changes. It will also help you see your particular flaws.
- Getting a video that shows the drills and swimming performed correctly lets you see exactly how you are to perform them. Most of the drills I suggest are in any good basic video on swimming; they are depicted in *Swimpower 2*, for example, exactly as we teach them at our clinics.

How to Videotape Yourself

The first choice is to shoot video of you swimming above and below the water both from the side and the front/back. However, underwater cameras and video-recording housing systems are not common household items as a video recorder usually is. To make the most of a surface-only video, shoot as follows:

1. Side view for two lengths while standing on the pool deck
2. Rear/front view for two lengths while standing on the pool deck
3. Rear/front view from a high point at the edge of the pool, such as a starting block or diving board, which will allow you to see some of the underwater pull

EQUIPMENT NEEDED FOR DRILLS

Short fins (preferably Zoomers) are the only piece of equipment you must have for technique work. Chapter 6 has a rundown of other useful and some not-so-useful swim toys. Fins are essential because they are needed for doing drills properly. The extra propulsion that they provide gives you a good body position during the drills. In addition, the fins help with making you more aware of your feet and legs, which helps you keep them in the slipstream of your body and not kick too big or too wide. Zoomers are best because they have a short blade, and this design provides a little propulsion but not so much that it allows the kick to get too big and come out of the slipstream.

The only drill you should not use fins on is the fist drill (Drill 10). In this particular drill it is advantageous to struggle a little. You will be forced to use your forearms to pull with so that you learn to bend the elbow early in the pull.

THE 10 ESSENTIAL FREESTYLE DRILLS

Every swimmer should know and practice the following 10 freestyle drills regularly. The first five focus on body position and rotation: improving the streamlined position. You will notice they are mostly kicking drills and involve little to no use of the arms. That is because you need to learn how to use your kick and core to rotate. This approach is not about kicking hard, but efficiently and in the correct fashion. The second set of five drills focuses on the arm cycle (often referred to as the *pull* or *stroke*). They will directly increase your propulsion. There is a definite reason for the order of the drills, as each one builds on the one before. So it is best to perform them in the suggested order.

Drills 1–5: Rotation, Body Position, and Kicking Drills

Drill 1: Vertical Kicking Drill

The purpose of this drill is to make the kick efficient and improve the long-axis rotation. From a vertical position with your arms at your sides, use a flutter kick to keep your head above the water. This is the part of the drill where you work on your kick. You can even look down at your legs and make sure that you are not bending the knees too much or bending forward at the waist. Utilize the upper muscles of the leg, and make small, fast movements. At first, this may be hard to do for even 30 seconds; work your way up to 1 minute.

Once you can comfortably perform the first part of the drill, start to work on your long-axis rotation. From the same vertical kicking position, rotate 90 degrees every 3 to 5 seconds to work on rotating from the kick and core. Rotate the entire body as a unit

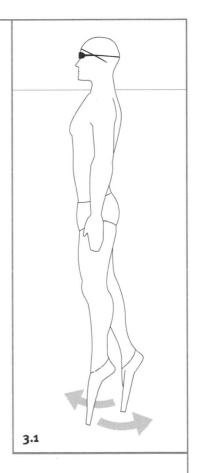

3.1

from the kick and hips 90 degrees to the right, and then back to center; then 90 degrees to the left, and back to center again. Repeat this for another minute. Focus on starting the rotation from the kick and hips, not the upper body. Figure 3.1 shows the vertical kick drill position.

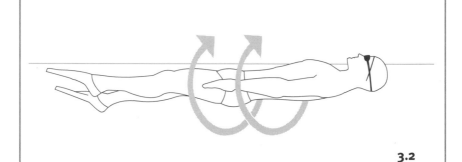

3.2

Drill 2: Corkscrew Drill

This drill will help you find a balanced and comfortable body position and work on your long-axis rotation. This is the same drill as vertical kicking, only we now move into the horizontal plane as we progress toward swimming.

Keep your hands at your sides, and again focus on turning the body from your kick and hips; do not lead with the head and shoulders. Unlike for vertical kicking, rotate your body 180 degrees so that you are either on your belly or on your back. Keep your head back and hips up to have an aligned body position when on your back. You should be looking at either the ceiling (when on your back) or the bottom of the pool (when on your belly). Be sure to take your time and breathe out when your head is facing down; when your head is facing up, try to relax and breathe normally. You can stay on your back and belly as long as you like until you feel ready to rotate properly. Be careful when reaching the end of the pool. Most pools have "warning" flags 5 yards from the wall to let you know that you are approaching the wall. In addition, many pool lane line colors switch to all red at the same point so you can see to your side and do not need to turn to look for the wall. See if your pool has these aids, and at that point you can roll over to your stomach and swim into the wall. If there are no such indicators at your pool, find a way to make sure you do not hit your head. Figure 3.2 shows the corkscrew drill.

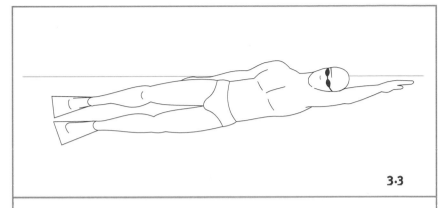

3.3

Drill 3: Kick-on-Side (KOS) Drill

This is one of the best drills for working on body position. The side position is one of the most streamlined forms a human can take. The objective here is to get comfortable with the head lying on the shoulder and having one goggle in and one out of the water. This is the ideal position for your head when you breathe.

Lie on your side with your bottom arm stretched out and ear pressing onto the shoulder. This arm should be just under the surface of the water with the hand parallel to the bottom of the pool. The top arm should be on your side. Do a flutter kick, and strive to maintain one goggle in and one goggle out of the water. The natural tendency is to start lifting the head to get the mouth out of the water to breathe. This actually makes you sink and work harder. If breathing while keeping a good head position is difficult, simply roll your head and look up, which should bring your mouth and nose out of the water to enable you to breathe. Do one whole length on one side and another length on the other. Figure 3.3 illustrates the KOS drill.

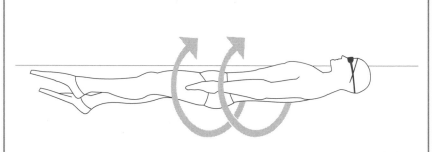

3.4

Drill 4: KOS Drill with One Stroke

This drill works the body position and also the rotation. We are again progressing toward swimming whole or regular freestyle. In this drill, you perform the KOS drill as described for Drill 3, and every 5 seconds or so you take a recovery with the trailing arm and pull with the leading arm as you rotate over to the other side. The focus here needs to be on making a smooth rotation and keeping the body in alignment. The best way to do so is to start the recovery first and stay on your side until your hand passes your face, and then start to bend the elbow of the leading arm. As the recovering arm enters the water, pull with the other arm and roll over to the other side. Keep your neck in alignment with your spine (do not lift the head) as though there is a long axis coming out the top of your head. Repeat over to the other side. Take your time; at first you may only do one rotation per length. Figure 3.4 illustrates the KOS with one stroke.

Drill 5: KOS Drill with Three Strokes

This drill also works the body position and rotation in another step toward full freestyle swimming. This drill is the same as the previous drill, with three strokes to rotate from one side to the other. Make sure to really focus on an integrated rotation on each stroke, driving it with your kick and hips, not the head and shoulders. This is the same figure as the one for Drill 4, since the only difference is that here you take three complete arm cycles, compared with one in the fourth drill.

Drills 6–10: Pulling Drills

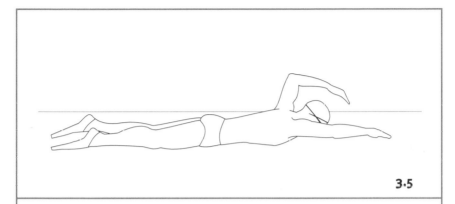

3.5

Drill 6: Catch-up Drill

This drill is great for working on making the exchange of one arm for the other in front of the head; this movement ensures that there is always an arm in front of the head to glide out on, which makes the body longer. In general, a longer body moves faster. (Think of the long hull design of speedboats.) In addition, the hands meeting in front of the head is a great reminder to pull and rotate. If you breathe on both sides, this drill can balance out your rotation. As you can see in Figure 3.5, you continue to glide out on the arm in front as you recover with the other arm.

When both arms are fully extended in front of your head, you then pull with the opposing arm. When first doing this drill, it is helpful to keep both arms in front of your head and kick a little while before switching arms. This gives you time to visualize a good pull with early elbow bending and good rotation during the power phase. As with all drills, take your time. The more slowly and accurately you do these drills, the more you will retain when you swim fast.

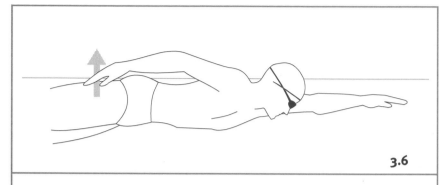

3.6

Drill 7: Catch-up Drill with Thumb Scrape

This is the drill that will ensure you finish each stroke. Before you push off, extend your arm down your leg and scrape your thumb on your thigh. At the finish of each pull, scrape your thigh in that same area. This is also the perfect drill for working on the release of the shoulder at the end of your stroke, since with the touch you are sensitized to that part of the stroke. The arrow in Figure 3.6 indicates the point where the arm pull (stroke) finishes and where the release (slight turnout of the palm) takes place.

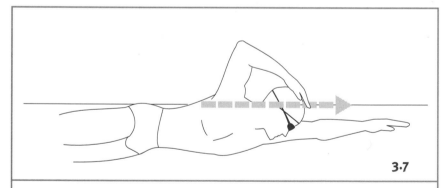

3.7

Drill 8: Catch-up Drill with Fingertip Drag

This twist on the catch-up drill is for focusing on the recovery and entry of your stroke. Here you want to lie on your side and slowly drag your fingertips through the water's surface as you recover. Ideally you should see the palm of your hand as it passes about 8 to 12 inches (20 to 30 centimeters) to the side of your head. Figure 3.7 shows that the fingertips stay in the water from the release phase of the stroke until the hand enters the water. After entry, the arm extends in front of the shoulder to full extension and meets the other outstretched arm.

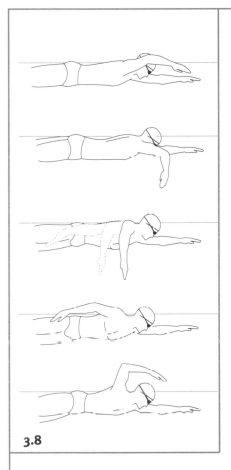

3.8

Drill 9:
Single-Arm Drill

This drill is used to work on all five phases of the stroke. It can be a tricky drill because of the fact that swimmers often try to work on all five phases at once, so the drill becomes a mess, accomplishing nothing. What invariably happens is that the swimmer makes the same mistakes in this drill as in his regular swimming. However, if you focus on only one aspect or phase for an entire two-length sequence (one arm in one direction, and the other coming back), the results are amazing. When in doubt of what to work on, focus on the early elbow bend at the beginning of the pull—something we can all improve. If you have had your swimming analyzed on video and can see in your mind's eye other flaws to correct, such as a poor entry or recovery, then do another two-length sequence focusing on just that phase.

Figure 3.8 shows the five phases of the arm cycle starting with the entry. This drill can be done with the nonstroking arm both in the front and at the back. The arm back is more advanced and actually works the rotation a little (more on that in Chapter 5). Remember, focus on improving only one at a time to maximize improvement.

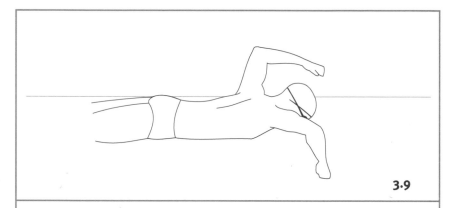

3.9

Drill 10: Fist Drill

This drill is specifically designed to help you develop the early elbow bend at the beginning of your stroke. Many swimmers get little to no benefit from this drill because they lack the knowledge of how to perform it correctly. This drill must be done slowly and with very conscious thought about feeling pressure on your forearm as you begin your pull. This sense of pressure is the feedback that indeed you are bending the elbow early enough to have the feeling of pressure on your forearm as you pull against the water.

What this drill does is take the hand out of the pull. In a sense, this forces you to bend the elbow to try to "catch" some water. If you rush the strokes, you will simply make the same errors you make in your regular swimming. In addition, I never have our swimmers do an entire length with fists. The dynamic feeling of opening the hands and feeling the added power from the higher elbow is the positive feedback that makes the change carry over to your regular stroke.

Because you actually need to struggle through the water a bit to feel this pressure on the forearm, it is best to do this drill without fins. This is the only drill where fins do not enhance the drill's effect. See Figure 3.9 and remember: Go slowly.

TIPS FOR PRACTICING DRILLS

This is by no means an end-all, be-all list of technique drills; however, it is a great foundation. Keep these tips in mind as you perform the drills:

- Use fins (preferably short) on all drills except the fist drill. The fins provide a little more speed to allow you to focus on the drill and not survival.
- Never skip drills. If you have to skip any part of the workout, go without a main set.
- Try to do 2 × 50 meters of each drill and 1 to 5 minutes of the vertical kick drill each practice.
- Use a set of "min/max 50s" once a month to play with your stroke efficiency. This is simply a set of 50s where you count your strokes and time yourself. Add the time and stroke count. That total now becomes your gauge of efficiency. Lower it. Create a PR (personal record), and play with speed and stroke length to see how low you can get that total of time and strokes. I recommend a set of 6 × 50 meters min/max at least once per month.

Just counting strokes can be misleading because you can get a very low stroke count by overgliding and delaying strokes. What happens is you become a slow swimmer who takes fewer strokes. For example, let's say you swim a 50-meter in 40 seconds and take 45 strokes; the total, then, is 85. On the next 50, you swim faster, going 35 seconds, and it takes 48 strokes, for a total of 83. Keep doing 50s, changing speeds and stroke rate to find the most efficient combination. As you improve your stroke, your PR on this drill will decrease. Have fun with it!

In addition to the fact that all swimmers stand to improve by doing these drills to "perfect" their own individual stroke, some areas of your swimming are probably really inefficient or sometimes even missing. A video analysis, as mentioned earlier, can usually show you what areas of your technique need more attention. If you have a straight arm pull, then an extra round of single-arm and fist drills will help. I have found that there are a few common flaws that swimmers make. Seeing any of these in your video analysis allows you to put your focus on these areas, either by performing specific drills or doing a combination of drills that allows you to start to make changes. A follow-up video analysis and new PRs in the min/max drill are helpful to gauge your success and assure you that your technique training is working.

THE MOST COMMON FLAWS IN FREESTYLE SWIMMING

As you can imagine, there are certain flaws that we humans seem to have a proclivity for in our technique. You may not have all of the following flaws, but my experience indicates that you probably have at least a few. Viewing a video of yourself will clearly show which you need to focus on the most. See directions on using video earlier in this chapter.

Poor Push-off

Figure 3.10 shows a poor push-off. For maximum speed off the walls, you need to have your arms squeezed together with one hand on top of the other. This reduces your frontal area and makes a more streamlined position.

Prescription: Do five streamlined push-offs and see how far you can glide on each one. Work at making yourself as narrow as possible.

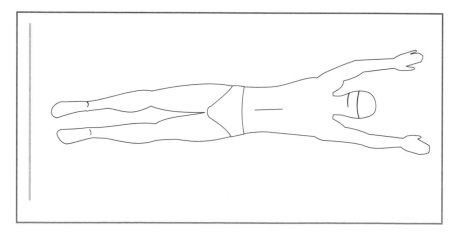

3.10 Poor Push-off

Hand/Arm Crossing an Imaginary Midline

This motion puts a tremendous amount of strain on the shoulder joint and makes your body "fishtail," or swing from side to side, creating drag. Figure 3.11 shows this flaw: Notice how the left hip goes left in reaction to the left arm crossing. The effect is literally a "dragging" of the lower body through the water.

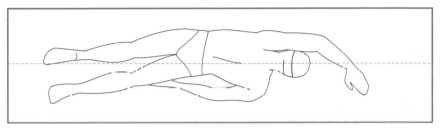

3.11 Hand/Arm Crossing an Imaginary Midline

Prescription: Do some single-arm and catch-up drills. At first you may feel like your arms are going in at the side of your body, really wide. That is simply because relative to where you were entering, it "feels" wide. Video is usually necessary to monitor progress on this flaw.

Early Entry

Figure 3.12 shows the effect of the early entry. The early entry is almost always followed by a diving down of the arm as opposed to an extending forward. The diving-down motion does not provide any "lift" (forces pushing the body up from the arm gliding forward parallel to the bottom of the pool) as the proper technique does; therefore, the body rides low in the water, and the swimmer takes faster strokes to try to stay afloat. It becomes a vicious cycle.

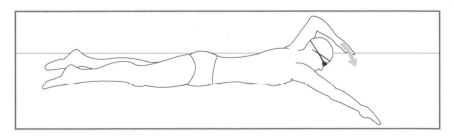

3.12 Early Entry

Prescription: Do the catch-up with the fingertip drag drill and the single-arm drill.

Short Finish

In Figure 3.13, it is clear that the swimmer is starting the recovery while the arm still has more distance to go to full extension. In sprinting, a shortened finish to increase the stroke rate is advantageous, but for distance swimming, full or almost full extension at the end of the pull phase is much more efficient.

Prescription: Do the catch-up drill with thumb scrape.

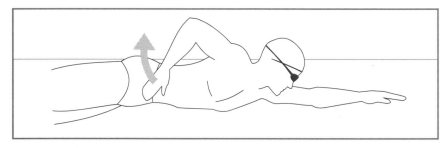

3.13 Short Finish

Dropping Elbow, Pressing Down on Pull

This motion robs swimmers of speed more than any other flaw. Figure 3.14 shows this very common flaw, which is actually part of an instinct that is no longer needed once swimming technique is understood. The arrow shows that the resultant force goes down as much or more than back. The forces sent down not only do not help you move forward but throw your body position off. A similar flaw with the same prescription is pulling with a straight arm; again much of the resultant force is directed down.

Prescription: Do the fist and single-arm drills.

No Long-Axis Rotation

This is also described as "flat swimming." This flaw shortens pull, reduces length of stroke, and creates more drag than what we observe in a swimmer with good rotation. Figure 3.15 shows a front

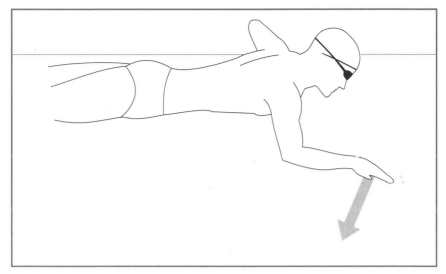

3.14 Dropping Elbow, Pressing Down on Pull

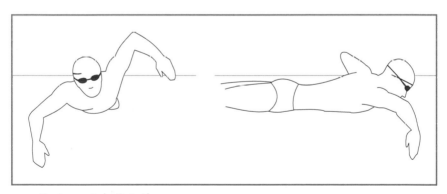

3.15 No Long-Axis Rotation

and a side view of a swimmer with no rotation. The little bit of rotation you see from the front view is simply the shoulder rotating in a circular pattern to allow the arm to come out of the water. This technique flaw puts a lot of stress on the shoulder for this reason.

Prescription: Do drills 1 through 5.

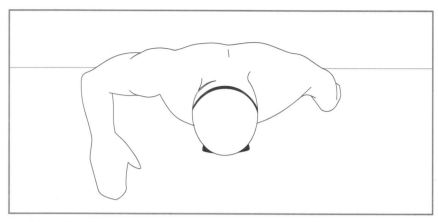

3.16 Head Too Low

Head Too Low

Figure 3.16 shows the head buried under the water. This position creates extra drag and makes sighting in open water more difficult.

Prescription: Do the catch-up drill. Work at the idea of letting the head "float" in the water.

Head Too High

The ideal head position when you are flat on your belly is the neck in line with the spine; in contrast, Figure 3.17 shows the flawed head position. As mentioned before, the most important time to worry about your head position is when you are on your side. The front head position is not as crucial, unless you lift or sink the shoulders with the head. Again, for that reason, a neutral head position where your neck is aligned with your spine is best.

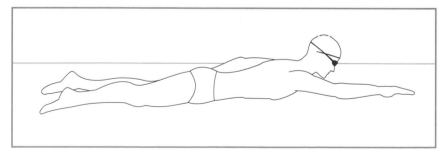

3.17 Head Too High

Prescription: Do the catch-up drill. Work on having your eyes look down at the bottom of the pool. Do some kick-on-side drills to remind you of where your head needs to be when you breathe.

Slapping and Overextending Entry

This flaw is usually caused by a swimmer's desire to get a long stroke. The long stroke needs to come from an extension just under the water; otherwise the extended arm over the water makes gravity push your body down. In addition, the slapping makes for loss of feel of the water and usually leads to a straight-arm pull. In Figure 3.18, you can see how that movement will make the swimmer's lower body sink. In addition, the swimmer will need to hurry up and take another stroke to stay afloat. Here again is one of those vicious cycles when the swimmer must use fast movements to keep up, and not really any significant force goes to moving forward.

Prescription: Perform the catch-up with fingertip drag and single-arm drills.

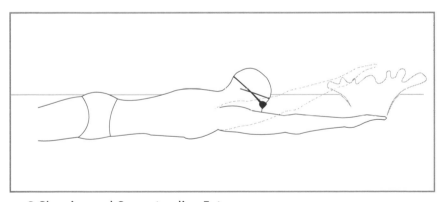

3.18 Slapping and Overextending Entry

DON'T JUST SWIM — SWIM SMART!

The biggest challenge is to do these drills correctly and effectively. Practicing the basics of off strokes is a terrific next step after you have begun to master these freestyle drills.

C H A P T E R

4 The Off Strokes

reestyle's status as the most popular style of swimming is high-lighted by the fact that swim coaches and swimmers usually refer to any stroke other than freestyle as one of the "off strokes." Although technically off strokes could include any-thing, even sidestroke or my girlfriend's favorite, the doggy paddle, for our discussion we are referring to backstroke, breaststroke, and butterfly. Together with freestyle, these four swimming styles (often referred to as *swimming strokes*) are the styles recognized for competitions.

WHY BOTHER WITH OFF STROKES?

Consider these three statements:

- Doing just a few 50s of backstroke and breaststroke each workout can help your freestyle by balancing your muscles, improving coordination, and giving your mind a mental break with new muscle patterns.
- Backstroke and breaststroke are helpful in open water for navigation and adjusting equipment such as caps and goggles.
- Practicing off strokes is a great way for you to develop a "feel for the water."

Swimmers and coaches use the phrase "a feel for the water" to describe a combination of being calm, relaxed, and aware (of where your body is and how it interacts with the water) while swimming. This feel for the water is a state of mind; in other sports, athletes describe being in the "flow state" or hitting a ball in "the sweet spot." All these states of mind have to do with a high level of skill and experience. Even after years of practice, entering and remaining in these states is not guaranteed; however, the more time you spend performing an activity, the more often you reach these high-level states.

Having a "feel for the water" is also used to describe the idea of finding "still" water. In other words, you want constantly to be pushing against water that you are not already moving. Time spent on these off strokes can speed up the process. For many swimmers, these strokes offer opportunities to get better awareness, especially in breaststroke and butterfly, because there is more of a conscious sculling motion than in freestyle. More on the "feel for the water" in Chapter 5.

WHAT DOES "IM" MEAN?

For many triathletes, *IM* stands for the ultimate long-distance triathlon, the Ironman. However, in the swimming world, *IM* stands for the individual medley, a swim race combining each of the four strokes. The common competition events are the 200- and 400-meter or yard IM. In an individual medley, the swimmer does an equal distance of butterfly, backstroke, breaststroke, and freestyle, in that order. Unless you were planning on competing in a swim meet in either the IM race or one of the three strokes other than freestyle, as a triathlete or fitness swimmer, practicing these strokes is not necessary; however, the benefits are worth the time and effort.

THE BASICS OF BUTTERFLY, BACKSTROKE, AND BREASTSTROKE

The same two physics principles that applied to freestyle apply to all strokes: reduce drag (improve body position) and increase power (propulsion). These two principles can be translated in a practical way to apply to our swimming:

- Streamlining to reduce drag is a constant principle and goal in all four strokes.
- Bending the elbow at a 90-degree angle at the beginning of the pull is paramount in maximizing propulsion for the pull in all four strokes.

We will not go into the same depth with the off strokes' basic techniques as we did with freestyle, but these technique primers will give you a solid foundation. If you have tried off strokes and feel intimidated, or if you have never tried these styles and are afraid, give them a try. My swimmers generally make quick progress and find that practicing off strokes enhances their progress in freestyle.

BACKSTROKE

The first off stroke to discuss is backstroke, because it is a nice balance to freestyle. Both backstroke and freestyle utilize long-axis rotation and the same flutter kick. Backstroke is the only stroke performed on your back. Because your face is out of the water all the time when you swim backstroke, there is no need to time your breathing. This position allows you to get into a nice breathing rhythm, and this easy breathing in turn helps you relax.

Working on the backstroke brings many benefits for triathletes and fitness swimmers. When in open water, for example, you can refit your goggles without losing forward motion. Often in an open-water swim, the sun is rising in front of you, which creates difficulty trying to navigate. Backstroke can help: By looking behind yourself and seeing the buoys or landmarks from where you left, you can see whether you are still on course. Finally, since backstroke is the only stroke on your back, it is great to do when swimming for a long time outdoors: You can even out your tan! (By the way, if swimming outside, you will probably need tinted goggles to protect your eyes from the sun.)

History

Interestingly, backstroke was a leisure stroke until the turn of the 20th century when it started to be used in a few competitions. The only rule then was to stay on your back, and it looked more like breaststroke on your back than its current look of freestyle on your back. With a few modern rule changes (allowance of a flip on the stomach at the end of each lap and underwater streamlined kicking), backstroke has attained almost the same speed as butterfly, making it the second fastest stroke.

Basic Technique

Learning to float on our back is a great way to start working on backstroke. Not everyone is buoyant enough to float easily, and if you're one of those people, simply use a light flutter kick to help keep you up.

The most common mistake in back floating and in backstroke is not having good posture. Bending the neck forward and "sitting" (hips down) makes it difficult to stay afloat and to streamline. Hips up and head back are two great things to keep in mind when starting to float and swim on our back.

Arm Cycle

The backstroke arm cycle: entry, elbow flexion, pull, and recovery. The phases are very similar to those in freestyle. One difference is that there is no release phase after the pull, because the arm and hand are in the correct position after the pull for the recovery.

Entry. The entry point for backstroke is in line with your shoulder. Your hand enters the water pinkie first, with the elbow straight (another distinction from freestyle). As your hand enters the water, it glides forward as your body rotates around the long axis. As you glide and rotate, your palm will face the bottom of the pool.

Elbow Flexion. As in freestyle, elbow flexion is very important. It provides a large paddle surface (hand and forearm) for maximum power. Long-axis rotation (as in freestyle) is the key to allowing for the bend in the elbow. Without this rotation, the forearm would come out of the water on your pull, or you would be forced to pull with a straight arm. A straight arm pull puts stress on the shoulder and provides much less propulsion. Keep extending your shoulder forward as you bend your elbow. This will make your stroke as long as possible.

Pull. As your hand passes your shoulder, start to extend your arm; use your triceps to finish the stroke, pushing your hand down. As in freestyle, backstroke uses a sculling motion that is aided by your rotation.

Recovery. This phase starts where the pull ends, with the thumb leading the way. As the arm passes the shoulder, you rotate your shoulder out; this movement turns the palm away from the body and prepares the hand for a pinkie finger entry.

The Kick
The kick in backstroke is a flutter kick, as in freestyle. Kicking on your back is an excellent balance to kicking on your stomach. The power of the kick comes mostly from the down kick. For this reason, freestyle uses more of the muscles in the front of the legs, whereas backstroke uses more of the muscles in the back of the legs.

Keys to Working on Backstroke

- Keep your hips up and head back. Most swimmers have a tendency to drop the hips and look down at the feet. This hampers rotation and creates excessive drag.
- As with freestyle, strive for a "neutral" neck, which means your eyes are looking straight up at the sky or ceiling.
- As you stroke, be sure to rotate the body from side to side (head stays stationary). This movement is the same long-axis rotation as in freestyle.

Backstroke Drills

- Kick on your back, working on the rotation from your core. You do this with your hands at your sides. Use your kick and core to rotate your body to the left; after your body comes back to neutral (flat-on-back position), use the kick and core to rotate the body to the right. Take a few kicks in the neutral position, and then repeat. This is a great drill for helping you learn to drive the long-axis rotation from your core and kick.
- Try single-arm backstroke. As with this drill for freestyle, you can work any aspect of the pull and rotation. Keep gliding

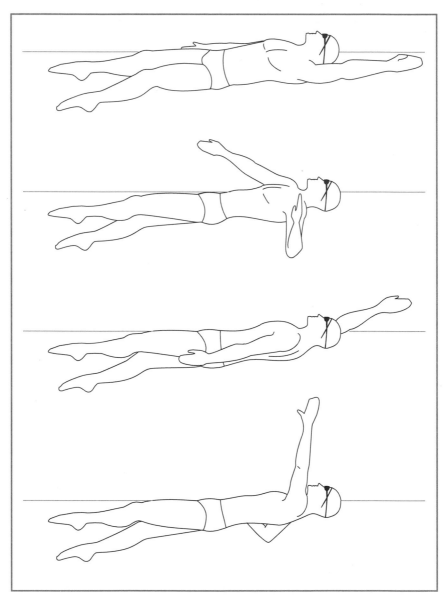

4.1 Backstroke: Integration of Backstroke Pull and Kick

with the arm going forward, and keep it there until you recover with the other arm to meet it. Study the pull in Figure 4.1, and work on one part of it at a time. Coordinate the pull with the rotation.

BREASTSTROKE

Breaststroke (like butterfly) uses an undulating motion to generate power, as opposed to the rotational power utilized in backstroke and freestyle. It is the most popular stroke after freestyle among fitness swimmers, because it allows the swimmer to see and breathe easily. Breaststroke is thus the most useful stroke when you are having trouble finding a landmark or buoy and want to keep some forward motion; it is easy to sight when swimming breaststroke since the head comes straight up while breathing. Its head-up position also makes breaststroke well suited to open-water swimming.

Triathlete Sheila Isaacs shows us just how efficient and suitable for open water breaststroke is. Sheila is an age group triathlete with two distinctions: She has done a triathlon in every state of the United States, and she only swims breaststroke. Even at the Ironman® Hawaii in 2004, Sheila had no problems making the cutoff time for a 2.4-mile swim. For her, breaststroke is faster than freestyle—a very rare occurrence since freestyle, done properly, is usually significantly faster and more efficient than breaststroke.

Breaststroke is considered to be a more relaxing stroke than the other three (don't say that to a competitive breaststroke swimmer). The head-up position allows for comfortable, normal breathing and the ability to see where you are going. Due to its long glide, breaststroke can be done with very little effort. The slowest of all four strokes (except for Sheila Isaacs!), breaststroke relies heavily on the kick and therefore develops the legs more than any other stroke.

Breaststroke's noncompetitive cousins are sidestroke and elementary backstroke. Sidestroke is a form of breaststroke performed on your side; elementary backstroke is breaststroke performed on your back. A connection similar to that between freestyle and backstroke exists between breaststroke and elementary backstroke. Many new swimmers find learning breaststroke easier than freestyle. If you feel awkward with freestyle, then try breaststroke as a stepping-stone.

History

Breaststroke is the oldest swimming stroke; sketches of a form of breaststroke have been found on Middle Eastern cave walls dating back to 9,000 B.C. It was a part of both the ancient Roman and Greek soldiers' military training.

When swim competitions were first conducted in England, they were held in harbors, and breaststroke was the style used. Due to innovative swimmers constantly improving the technique, breaststroke has gone through many changes and had to be saved from extinction as a competitive stroke at least three times. First, around the turn of the 20th century, the invention of the crawl (freestyle) temporarily caused breaststroke to disappear from competition. Eventually breaststroke was defined as its own stroke. Next, in the 1930s, breaststroke was temporarily sidelined by the new stroke, butterfly. At the time, butterfly entailed a breaststroke kick with butterfly arms. Eventually rule changes made butterfly the fourth and final stroke. After that, the Japanese discovered that they could swim breaststroke faster underwater. Eventually, in 1957, the rules were changed to allow only one kick and pull underwater.

Breaststroke is still undergoing many changes, and currently the "wave breaststroke" is the standard for competition because it's the fastest version of the stroke. The wave breaststroke utilizes an over-water recovery (elbows must stay in water). This recovery does two things: It decreases drag due to the reduced resistance of recovery in the air, and it lifts the body higher, utilizing an undulation motion to get more power for the glide.

The rules for breaststroke (as with the other strokes) are constantly changing as swimmers invent new variations. Competitive swimming's governing body must decide whether each change will become a part of "legal" breaststroke or will become a movement that could disqualify a swimmer. Despite this, the ancient art of breaststroke has stood the test of time.

Basic Technique

Arm Cycle
The breaststroke arm pull has four parts: recovery, elbow flexion, pull, and inward sweep.

Recovery. To begin the recovery, place your hands in a praying position, palms facing each other, just under your chin. As you drive your arms forward, keep your hands together. As the arms start to reach full extension, turn your palms down.

Elbow flexion. As in freestyle, this part is very important. After turning the palms down, bend your arms at the elbows and sweep them out toward the outside of your shoulders. Your hands should be constantly adjusting to be perpendicular to the direction of limb movement. This advice sounds more complicated than it is. As you sweep out, your hand angle pitches to make the resultant force backward and hence propel you forward.

Pull. This phase is where you generate power and pull your upper body slightly out of the water to allow you to breathe and get the hips up for a powerful kick. This movement is similar to the freestyle pull, but it is a half pull and ends when your arms get to the shoulders. The elbows stay bent throughout the breaststroke pull. Make sure you bend the elbows as you pull, and only pull back as far as your chest.

Inward sweep. At the end of the pull, sweep your arms in and prepare for the recovery.

The Kick

Starting from a straight-leg streamlined position, draw your knees up toward your chest, and then push your legs out, back, and in. There are two main movements: bringing the legs up and bending the knees, and pushing out together and back for the thrust. This kick differs from all other kicks in swimming because it takes place in the horizontal plane, moving laterally. All other kicks are in the vertical plane, moving up and down. It is important to get the timing right between the pull and the kick; otherwise you end up fighting against yourself (see Figure 4.2).

Keys to Working on Breaststroke

- The breaststroke is the only stroke that does not allow full recovery over the water, so a full pull would cost too much in drag to get the arms back to the beginning of the next pull.
- Make sure to squeeze your legs together (as you throw your arms forward) at the finish of the kick to provide maximum propulsion and a streamlined position.
- Work on getting the timing between the pull and the kick correct, so you get a little glide after the kick in a streamlined (arms and legs together) position.

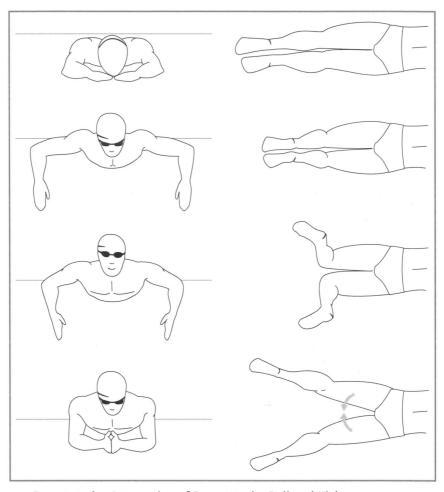

4.2 Breaststroke: Integration of Breaststroke Pull and Kick

Breaststroke Drills

- A great drill is to do a butterfly kick with fins and the breast-stroke pull. This combination helps work the kick for the butterfly and gets the undulating motion of the hips into your breaststroke.
- Do the double-kick drill: Make two kicks to every pull, which allows you to work on the froglike kick of breast-stroke and focus on really squeezing the legs together at the end of the kick.

BUTTERFLY

Arguably the most beautiful stroke, butterfly has been compared to a dolphin undulating in the water; hence, another common name for this stroke is dolphin butterfly or simply dolphin. It is also a very powerful stroke and the hardest swimming style to perfect. It allows you to really work your core muscles, building them stronger than you can with the other strokes. Butterflyers are usually more muscular than other swimmers. Lap for lap, butterfly will give you the workout of your life. Fly, as it is often called, is also a great way to work on your streamlined position.

One of the reasons I like to see athletes do some butterfly in training is that, because it's the most strenuous stroke, it makes freestyle seem really easy by comparison. What's great for training, however, may not be great for triathlon competition.

In the early days of my triathlon career, I thought about how cool it would be to finish the triathlon with some butterfly. While I may have looked cool doing fly at the finish of the swim, I looked pretty silly when five guys ran past me in the transition area while I gasped for air!

History

Not many people know that butterfly is actually an outgrowth of breaststroke. As breaststroke was developing in the 1930s, swimmers started to swim it with the butterfly arms (retaining the breaststroke kick) and swam faster. For a few years, this version actually replaced conventional breaststroke. In the 1950s, a rule made breaststroke a separate stroke, specifying that the recovery had to be under the water. Butterfly was born, and soon the dolphin kick was added, making the stroke very fast. Recognized officially in 1952, butterfly has a relatively short history. That is only 20 years before Mr. Fly himself, Mark Spitz, crushed his competitors at the 1972 Munich Olympics.

Basic Technique

In addition to the undulating dolphin kick, the butterfly uses a powerful sweeping arm cycle resembling (not surprisingly) the wings of a butterfly.

Arm Cycle

The arm action in butterfly is similar to that in freestyle; however, the in-and-out sweeping motion of the arms is no longer facilitated by the rotation since fly is swum without long-axis rotation. Therefore, attention must be paid to sweeping the arms out and in when pulling. The four phases of the arm cycle in fly are entry, elbow flexion, pull, and recovery.

Entry. The fly entry is like freestyle, but both arms are together. You use your shoulder rotation and undulating motion to extend the arms forward. Due to the undulating motion, the arms are at almost full extension upon entry.

Elbow flexion. This movement is identical to freestyle's elbow flexion. Try to keep the elbows as high as possible to prepare for the pull to come. Start to sweep the arms out slightly as you bend the elbows.

Pull. This is where you need to consciously sweep the arms out, in and out again. This motion makes an hourglass figure (see Figure 4.3).

Recovery. The recovery is similar to freestyle's, but with less elbow bend. At the end of the pull, it is important to rotate your shoulders outward to open up the shoulder joints for the recovery. The timing of your breathing and recovery needs to be such that your head drops back into the water as your arms come past your shoulders. This allows for greater glide upon entry.

Keys to Working on Butterfly

- Do not lift your head any higher than you need to when breathing, and use your kick and hip action to help you generate power and bring your head up and forward for the breath.
- Drop your head as soon as you have gotten your air.
- Keep the legs together and kick from your core.
- A helpful tool for learning how to do the undulating motion in butterfly is a monofin (see Chapter 6).

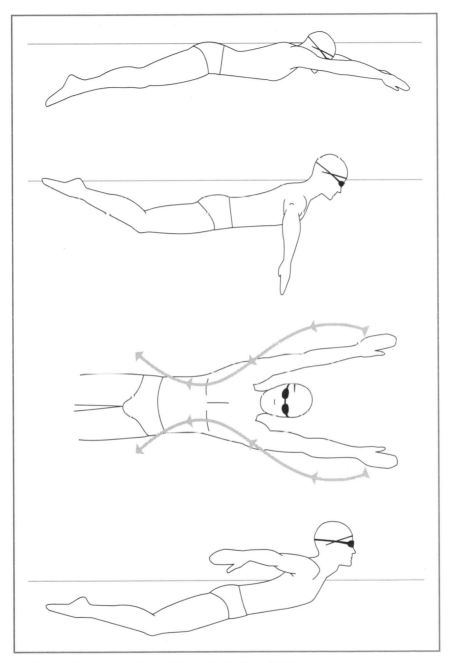

4.3 Butterfly: Integration of Butterfly Pull and Kick

Butterfly Drills

- A good butterfly starts with a good kick. A great way to practice this is to do a few lengths (with rest in between) of kick underwater in a streamlined position. The key is to use your core and learn to undulate to create power.
- The single-arm fly is a good drill to do in combination with the kick because it works on the arm action of butterfly without being as strenuous as regular butterfly. I suggest using Zoomer fins on both these butterfly drills.

OFF STROKE TRAINING

To incorporate the off strokes into your training, either do a few 50s of each stroke at all practices or have one day a week (or every other day) as "IM day." On IM day you would do all or part of the main sets off strokes (any stroke other than freestyle). Although you could do all backstroke, all breaststroke, or all butterfly on these days, it is best to do sets of IM alternated with freestyle.

For example, try 6 × 200s (or 100s), alternating freestyle and off stroke with 30 seconds' rest between, or a 200 IM. A 200 IM is a 200 in which you do a 50 of each stroke: butterfly, backstroke, breaststroke, and freestyle. For many swimmers, however, fly is so strenuous that a 50 is really pushing it; in that case, we have swimmers do 100 IMs so there is only one length of fly at a time.

CHAPTER

5 Advanced Freestyle Techniques

Make sure you have spent at least a month or two on the basics set forth in Chapters 2 and 3 and feel very comfortable with your freestyle and your improvement thus far, because the advanced techniques taught here will be difficult to master without a solid foundation. In fact, these techniques will probably slow down your progress without the basics. I see this problem with many swimmers. They get excited after learning a few basics, and then they read about some new high-level technique and try to implement it. However, their foundation is not strong enough, and they lose whatever foundation that they had established.

These advanced techniques require you to be relaxed. An awareness of your body in the water is essential. In addition, these techniques are best suited for faster swimmers. By "faster swimmers," I am referring to swimmers who can swim an all-out 100-meter freestyle in less than 1 minute, 20 seconds—about 1 minute, 12 seconds for 100 yards.

BREATHING PATTERNS

Breathing patterns were explained in depth in Chapter 2, but now that you have advanced, it is time to refocus on this swimming component to see whether you need some adjustments. Even for the advanced swimmer, a continuous focus on relaxing and full exhalation will yield the best improvement.

Do most of your training with breathing to alternate sides (every three or five strokes), which will help you develop a balanced stroke in terms of rotation. Always use whatever pattern is most comfortable when racing or doing a key fast set. You will likely find out that you have a breathing pattern for warming up, another for race pace, and a third for sprinting. As your intensity increases, your need for oxygen increases, and so does your stroke rate; therefore, you have less time between strokes than when going slow. So many individual factors are involved that a formula of how many breaths to take is not possible.

I notice that when I am in better shape, my body processes oxygen more efficiently and I am able to breathe less. The advantage to breathing less is that you are more streamlined and there is a little less lag to the side on which you are breathing.

Breathing as little as possible is most important in sprint swimming, where tenths of seconds are huge. What is a sprint of this nature? A race with all-out, 100 percent effort for any distance of 100 meters/yards or less. In this case, it is actually an advantage to take as few breaths as possible because no matter how much you breathe, the intensity of the effort will make you go anaerobic (producing energy without oxygen). When you go anaerobic, your cells are producing lactic acid (a waste product of cellular energy production) at a faster rate than they can process it. When lactic acid reaches certain levels in the muscles, they ache, and you soon will need to slow down or stop. Part of the training in sprint freestyle, then, is teaching the body and mind to handle and buffer these high levels of lactic acid.

Prescriptions:

- Try a breath control swim: Do a long, straight swim, starting with breathing every two strokes and adding a stroke per breath each length. Length 2 would be breathing every three strokes, length 3 every four, and so forth, until you can do an entire length without breathing. After the no-breathing length, go backward, subtracting one stroke each length from the breathing pattern until you finish at two strokes per breath. This is a great way to work on controlling your breathing. I have my advanced swimmers do this twice: once easy, then for time. This exercise helps you see which breathing pattern is the most efficient for you.

- Meditation and yoga are excellent ways to work on breath control outside the water. These techniques often translate into enhanced and deeper breathing while swimming.

DISTANCE SWIMMING VERSUS SPRINT SWIMMING

Our focus to this point has been long-distance techniques. It is valuable to note that distance freestyle and sprint freestyle are practically two different strokes. The length of your stroke becomes less important than your turnover (stroke rate) when you are sprinting. In addition to increasing the stroke rate, you will have to sacrifice some of your long-axis rotation and the finish of your pull. This style is not the most efficient way to swim longer distances; however, it is more powerful and faster. The problem is that it can only be sustained for shorter distances because the increased stroke rate, reduced efficiency (shorter strokes), and anaerobic effort (effort is too intense to utilize oxygen) will put you into oxygen debt and "anaerobia" (my own term for the state your body is in when you go from aerobic to anaerobic). If you are a distance swimmer or triathlete, this message may read to you like a sign that says, "Stay away from sprinting!" Nothing could be further from the truth.

Sprinting, or simply very fast swimming, needs to be a part of every swimmer's training—yes, even fitness swimmers. The body adapts to change. If you always swim slowly, you will get used to that pace, and a few things happen: You lose fitness, you get slower, and your technique deteriorates. Working on your speed becomes very important for distance swimmers because you need to experience a speed before you can maintain it. For example, if you want to hold a pace of 1:30 for 100 meters in a 1,500-meter swim, you need to know what 1:30 feels like. If you train at 1:40 all the time, you will never be able to hold 1:30. As a matter of fact, for this particular goal, doing a set of five 100-meter swims holding 1:20 is more helpful than doing a set of ten 100-meter swims holding 1:30.

Another example of the "need for speed" in an open-water race is when the first buoy is 50 meters away. A lot of swimmers will be at that buoy. Getting there ahead of the masses may end up saving you minutes on a long swim by avoiding collisions and putting you in a faster swim group. Similarly, you may find in the middle of a swim that you are in a "pack" that is too slow for you, but the group ahead is 25 meters away, and the distance is growing. If you have a sprint speed developed, you can sprint up to that group.

I learned this lesson the hard way in 1993 at the Ironman® Hawaii. Being a good swimmer (sprinter in high school and college), I figured my training time was best spent biking and running. My swim training consisted of long medium-speed swims, with no speed work. Halfway through the swim portion of the race, I was leading a pack of about five swimmers when I noticed the lead pack about 40 meters ahead and pulling away. I knew I could stay in that pack if I could just bridge the gap. No problem—after all, I was a sprinter! The key word here is *was*. When I started to go, I could only close the gap about halfway before I started to fade. I tried valiantly three times, and all I received for my effort was a world of lactic acid. I did the remaining mile of the swim in "no man's land," that area where you are in between groups and getting no draft (more on drafting in Chapter 7) or energy from other swimmers. The lead pack pulled away and finished 2 minutes, 30 seconds faster than I. They certainly used less energy as well. My time was okay, 53 minutes, but it could have been 50:30. Worse than the time loss was the fact that I was so wasted after the effort in the water that my first 10 miles on the bike was a recovery, not the way you want to start a 112-mile bike ride.

Needless to say, I learned my lesson. I always try to keep up at least some speed training for myself and our athletes. If you don't, then don't try to sprint in a race. Remember, you must have the tool and the experience practicing with it before you can take the tool out and use it effectively. A piece of equipment that helps you systematically and quantifiably work on your stroke rate is the Tempo Trainer (more on this device in Chapter 6).

Prescription. A fun—and effective—set to do is half-pool sprints. Simply do an all-out sprint with no breaths for approximately 12.5 meters/yards, and then immediately go into long easy strokes with breathing to get to the end of the 25. Take a full recovery, and repeat 8 to 16 times. The key is to go totally crazy on the superfast part, and keep the effort well under 10 seconds. Your turnover should go way up, and your rotation will reduce (i.e., you will swim flatter). Your stroke will shorten, and your technique will look sloppy. All of these effects are okay. The purpose of this drill is to get the stroke rate up. For efforts under 10 seconds, the body uses the creatine phosphagen (CP) system, which is subanaerobic. This means you do it for such

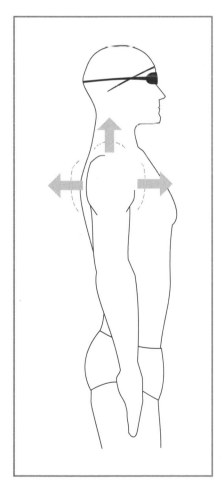

5.1 Shoulder Rotation

a short time that you do not get a chance to build up lactic acid. The CP system can be trained effectively in a few weeks. I generally use this approach with my swimmers to prep them for a race or a key set where I want them to have some speed. It is not uncommon for our swimmers to average a few seconds per 100 faster after a set of these half-pool sprints than the same set without them.

SHOULDER ROTATION

We discussed the long-axis rotation that takes place in efficient freestyle. Another rotation that is very natural is the shoulder rotation. This is a circular or oval rotation of the shoulder joint very similar to a forward shoulder shrug. Figure 5.1 shows how the shoulder should move as you go through your arm cycle.

One of the main benefits of good shoulder rotation is that it lengthens the entry and extension of your stroke (see the arrow pointing up in the figure). In addition, the right and left arrows in Figure 5.1 show how the rotation helps keep the shoulder open and free during the arm cycle, thus helping prevent shoulder injury.

Prescriptions:

- Do a few (two sets of 10) forward shoulder shrugs with low or no weights on dry land before swimming to familiarize yourself with the movement you want to have in your swimming. This move is also quite helpful to do in reverse for backstroke—another example of how backstroke balances and complements freestyle.
- Try the single-arm drill with your leading arm at your side. This is a variation of the single-arm drill described in Chapter 3. With your arm back, you can feel the movement of your shoulder as you do this drill. Do at least two 50s; each 50 is a 25 with one arm and another 25 with the other.

SCULLING AND THE S-PULL PATTERN

One of the more interesting aspects of swimming in general and freestyle specifically is the notion of sculling and the S-pull pattern. I have found that for almost all swimmers (especially beginners), the idea of the arm making an S pattern when they pull and are trying to rotate the body at the same time becomes an exercise akin to circling the arms in two different directions or doing the childhood game of one hand patting the head and one hand rubbing the tummy while chewing gum. That complexity is why in Chapter 2 we stressed the long-axis or body rotation, which comes naturally with good rotation, more than the S-pull pattern. Some advanced freestyle swimmers, however, can increase their power by fine-tuning the sculling and pull pattern.

Sculling and the S-pull pattern go hand in hand. Sculling is the movement of a limb from side to side to create lift, similar to how a propeller works. Figure 5.2 shows that as the hand pulls back, it is also moving side to side. This is the same movement we discussed in treading water. In a sense you are generating propulsion

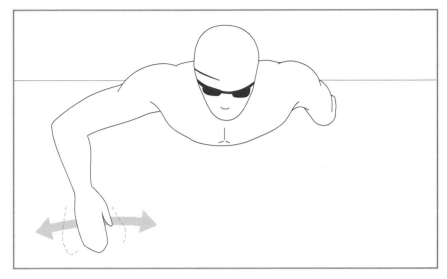

5.2 Sculling

in two ways: forces going straight back and forces created going back by sculling.

The S pattern of pulling shown in Figure 5.3 depicts how the arm sweeps out first, then in and out again as you pull back. This is helpful in creating more power for two reasons: First, as your hand moves to the side, it finds "still" water; therefore, you get a better "grip" as you pull back. Second, as the hand–forearm combination moves side to side, you are creating a sculling motion, which adds to your power generation.

These are subtle and individual techniques. It is unnecessary to utilize both principles because, as we have shown, they are each included in the other, and the long-axis rotation enhances and creates this effect as well. The point is that now you are at a point in your swimming to experiment and fine-tune. Visualizing these principles with the help of the following prescriptions will help you move toward that "perfect" individual stroke.

Prescriptions:

- Try this sculling drill: Do an easy kick on your stomach, and use a sculling motion with both hands at three positions to

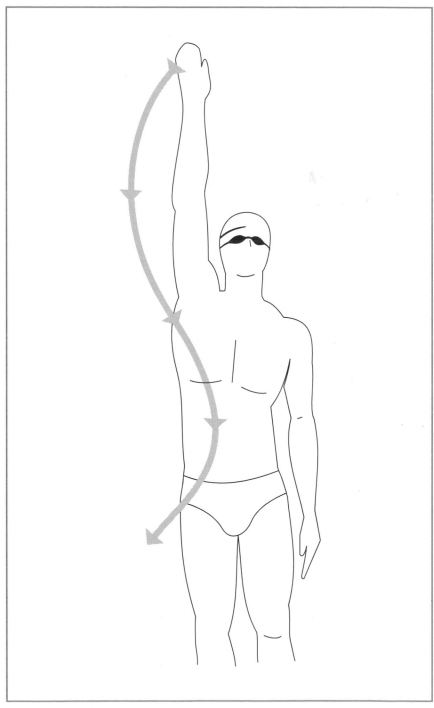

5.3 S-pull Pattern

complete a three-length sequence. First perform the sculling with the arms in the "catch" phase. Next perform sculling with the arms in the middle of the pull phase. Finally, perform sculling at the finish of the pull.

- Do the S-pull drill. This is simply a single-arm drill, as described in Chapter 3, with the emphasis on taking the arm through an S-like path using your long-axis rotation.

KICKING PATTERNS

Similar to a "stroke" in the arm movement in swimming, we have a "beat" when referring to the kick. Just as every time the arm enters the water we count a stroke, each time the foot goes down we count a beat. There are three distinct kicking patterns in freestyle: the two-beat, four-beat, and six-beat kicks.

By far the most common is the two-beat kick. It is the kick used for easy and long-distance swimming. The six-beat kick is used for fast swimming. We used to never see this kick in distance swimming, but in recent years many distance swimmers have trained so well that they can either use the six-beat kick in spurts during a long race or even maintain it for the entire race.

If a six-beat kick is faster than a two-beat, why not use it all the time? It costs too much. The leg muscles are the largest muscles in the body and therefore require the most amount of oxygen and blood. When you employ a six-beat kick, you are using large amounts of oxygen. Because the speed increase from a six-beat kick is small and the cost (in terms of human energy) is high, it only makes sense to use it sparingly. Keep in mind, too, that a proper (low-intensity) two-beat kick is paramount to an efficient freestyle because it aids in rotating and keeping the legs up, thereby reducing drag.

The four-beat kick is much less common and is sometimes done with a crossover kick. It is not as efficient as a two-beat and less powerful than a six-beat. Someone who does this kick generally has poor rotation and is fishtailing through the water. This is basically a six-beat kick, but because of poor rotation, the swimmer's lower body lags the upper body, and the legs cross at the ankles for two beats to allow the legs to catch up with the upper body. If you find you have a crossover kick, you will need to refocus on long-axis rotation. Work on developing your efficient two-beat and fast six-beat kicks during the vertical kick and kick-on-side drills.

Prescription: At the end of a vertical kicking drill, kick as fast as you can and see how high you can get your body to come out of the water. This technique will help you develop a strong six-beat kick.

Dolphining

A kick-related pool technique that involves the legs is dolphining (from a dive and off the wall). Probably one of the most significant developments in swimming has to do with what is done at the dive and at the turns. This is not a new concept. In the 1950s, a Japanese breaststroker competed in a breaststroke race and won, doing the entire race underwater! It seems the turbulence of the body at the surface of the water is considerably higher than in a streamlined form completely submerged. The rules were adjusted to say that breaststrokers were allowed only one pull and one kick each length to be performing "legal" breaststroke. As you will see in the following story, it took an experimenting college backstroker to find out that with the proper undulating or "dolphining" off the wall or starting blocks, one could maintain most of the speed and be much faster without using one's arms.

It started back in the early 1980s with a Harvard backstroker named David Berkoff. He would do almost the entire first length underwater, kicking with a dolphin motion on his back. When he popped up, he was more than a body length ahead of everyone, and essentially the race was over. This start became known as the "Berkoff Blast-off." It was so dramatic that eventually a rule was added to say that a swimmer had to come up within 15 meters or be disqualified.

More recently, swimmers have started to use this technique in sprint butterfly and freestyle off the dives and walls. The reason for its use after dives and turns is that a good push-off or dive makes you travel so fast that the drag of coming out of the slipstream to start pulling actually slows you down.

The results of dolphining are incredible. At the 2004 NCAA Men's Championships, Ian Crocker of Texas broke the world record for the 100-meter (short-course) freestyle twice in one day. It was so amazing to see him turn together with seven other swimmers and then dolphin off the last turn and the race was over—he was a body length ahead and broke his own world record from the morning by almost a second. I noticed that in the preliminaries, Ian had not used the dolphining technique, but apparently he decided to save it for the finals. A serious drawback to this technique is that it uses lots of muscle power, which explains why no distance swimmers utilize it. No surprise, too, to find out that freestyle is not Ian's best stroke—butterfly is.

You may never use dolphining, but practicing it is a blast. No wonder dolphins always look like they are smiling—going fast is fun!

Prescription: Do a few 25-meter/yard sprints, starting with a dolphining glide. You will need a decent amount of rest at each wall (at least 20 seconds) due to the anaerobic effect and large muscle recruitment aspect of this technique. Practice dolphining first with fins. Try a monofin to really get the feel of this undulating motion.

GETTING A "FEEL FOR THE WATER": ADVANCED ARM CYCLE TECHNIQUES

That elusive "feel for the water" is described by many coaches and swimmers differently. What one swimmer needs to feel effective in the water may be very different from another's. This is a personal experience. However, as always, we can learn a lot by listening to how skilled swimmers describe the feeling they get when they feel they are the most effective or "on" while swimming.

My favorite description of "a feel for the water" comes from Rip Esselstyn. Rip is arguably one of the most accomplished swimmers and triathletes in the world. A national-level swimmer in high school and college, including racing in the 1984 Olympic Trials, he continued to swim as a professional triathlete. In his 20-year career, Rip has been first out of the water in just about every major event, including multiple times at the St. Croix Half Ironman® and the Escape from Alcatraz triathlon. Recently Rip was first out of the swim at the XTERRA World Championships in Maui, at age 40!

More than once Rip and I have spent a few days together preparing for the XTERRA championship race by doing daily open-water swims. He literally transforms each day as he gets closer and closer to getting his "stroke back" and reconnecting with his feel for the water. His focus is not at all on effort but on tactile sensations that have to do with timing and angles of attack of his pull. I also believe at some level he is fine-tuning the coordination and timing of the pull with his breathing and kicking. Even for a veteran swimmer like Rip, the feeling he is after is not readily available to him; he needs to work at it. This is how he describes how he feels when he is in his most effective swimming state: "a feeling of leveraging my power, by utilizing the back muscles (mostly lats) with a bend in the elbow at the beginning of the stroke." He also describes a feeling of continuous exchange of the arms in the beginning of the pull. He demonstrates on land by alternating each arm in front and having one "catch" as the other is coming forward.

My interpretation is that Rip is describing a very front end–dominated style, meaning much more focus is placed on the beginning of the arm cycle than on the end. It is interesting to note that even though Rip's focus is not on a long stroke and a good finish, his pulls are still quite long and go to almost a full extension. I also noticed that, as in my own stroke, an acceleration takes place during the pull that aids in this connection. It becomes an experiment of the pacing and timing of the pull, for each arm alone and for each arm in relation to the other arm.

Intellectually, Rip knows quite a bit about stroke mechanics, but that is not what he thinks about when he prepares for events. He works on getting into the flow and letting those movements come naturally. I offer this story so that you get an idea of how to go about finding your own way to develop and then foster your feel for the water. Realize that this process will be slightly different for each swimmer and each style.

SHORTENING THE FINISH OF THE PULL

One of the newest hot topics in swimming these days is the idea of not finishing the pull so that you can get the arms around faster and get back to the power phase faster. Although this approach has some merit, it has thwarted the improvement of many beginning swimmers, who first need to learn long efficient strokes before learning how to maximize their power. I have seen way too many swimmers who do not have an efficient front end to their stroke start to play with this technique with a resultant stroke that looks like a crab being held in the air.

Because you are ready to try this high-level technique, do a set of min-max (described in Chapter 3) drills playing with a (very slightly) shorter finish. Do not forget to rotate your hand out (the release) as it comes out of the water to protect your shoulder.

Prescriptions:

- Do the catch-up drill with a focus on accelerating the pulls. The pacing of the arm cycle should be fairly slow and easy for the recovery, entry, and elbow bend, and then accelerate through the pull phase. When brought into your regular swimming, "almost catch-up" swimming will help foster the front end–dominated stroke that Rip describes.
- Do a 6 × 50 min/max, playing with these new techniques and going for a new PR.
- Use music, meditation, yoga, stretching, and swim-specific strength training to facilitate an optimal mind–body connection.
- Let go of your focus on technique and simply play with rhythm and breathing.

FLIP TURNS

As a swimming coach, I am frequently asked, "Should I bother with flip turns?" Although not a requirement for your enjoyment of swimming, flip turns can really make a difference in your performance. They are not for competitive pool swimmers only. Fitness swimmers, triathletes, and open-water swimmers all derive great benefit from training with flip turns.

Here are my reasons for learning and using flip turns:

- They make your swimming more continuous, whereas doing an open turn is basically stopping and starting every time you get to the end of the pool.

- They are faster.
- They look really cool and send off the signal "Yes, I am a swimmer!"
- Learning and perfecting the flip turn is challenging and quite rewarding.
- Nothing is more frustrating than when you are swimming faster than someone, then she flips at the wall while you do an open turn, so she is now a half body length ahead.

Okay, how do you do it? There are three phases to a flip turn: the approach, the flip, and the push-off. The best way to learn the flip turn is to master one phase at a time.

The first phase, the approach, is the easiest. It will take you some time to learn to gauge where you should take your last stroke. This position varies for each swimmer depending on his or her height, arm length, speed, glide, and efficiency. The only way to learn it is through trial and error. Start by flipping a little further from the wall or even in the middle of the pool and get progressively closer.

Most pools have crosses on the bottom and on the wall. These markings are helpful, but realize that not all pools are standard with them, so you need to get used to each pool. What you should really focus on is the wall. You will need to lift your head slightly from the "ideal" head position as you approach the wall. After you judge your last stroke and have both arms at your sides, you are ready for the second stage.

The middle phase, the flip itself, is actually a somersault performed while moving forward. This is the phase that most people have trouble with. If this movement is hard for you to master, you can practice by performing somersaults in the water from a standing position. Tuck your head and roll in a ball. When you actually do the flip turn, you will open up your legs more than when you practice the somersault. Your feet should be shoulder-width apart as they come over your body. You should also pike your body by bending at the waist at a 90-degree angle.

For the final phase, push off while on your back, and, as you come off the wall underwater, roll over onto your stomach. Remember to streamline as you push off so that you can carry some good speed into the next lap. This technique is referred to as the "flat" flip turn. Remember to breathe out during the flip and push-off (see Figure 5.4).

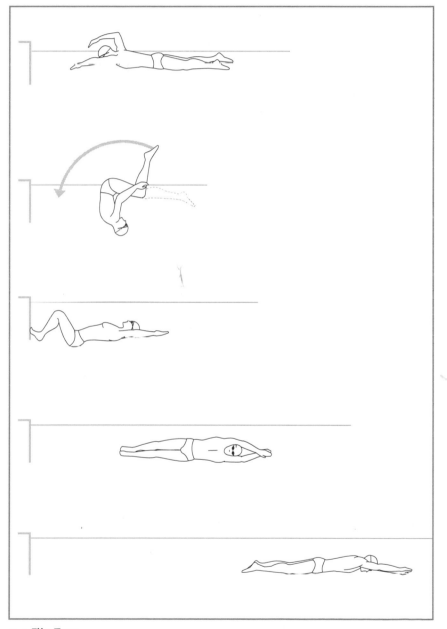

5.4 Flip Turn

Flip turns are difficult to master. Many swimmers fear cracking their heels on the wall, running out of air, or getting water up the nose. Remember, flip turns are not mandatory, so take the pressure off yourself. If you fear hitting the wall, realize that when swimmers mess up on the flip turns they usually flip too early and "miss it." When a swimmer says he missed a turn, he means he flipped and missed touching the wall. If you get water up the nose, you are either not breathing out or breathing out so fast that halfway around the flip no more air is being exhaled. The key to a smooth flip turn is to take a deep breath as you approach the wall, and then exhale slowly and steadily as you flip.

I can remember my first flip as if it were yesterday. I was about 12 or 13 years old, and an older swimmer named Jay was showing me how to learn the flip. We went through all the stages that I've described. I was finally ready to do one at the end of the pool. I stroked, did a nice approach, did my flip, and had a nice streamlined push-off. But when I stopped and stood up in the water, something felt weird. Jay said, "Nice job!" Then he saw the strange look on my face and asked, "Are you okay?" Two jet streams of water came shooting out of my nose! We laughed, and he shared with me that the same thing happened to him when he learned. Within a few more tries, I learned how to meter out my exhale and was flipping like crazy.

A great thing about flip turns is that you can adjust them on the fly. If you end up too close to the wall, you can just ball up. If you end up too far away, you can open up your legs a bit and allow your momentum to carry you to the wall.

Finally, the most important thing about learning to do good flip turns is practice. Commit to a finite number of flip turns each practice, and increase that number each practice. Do not be discouraged by missing a flip here and there. Even accomplished swimmers miss turns.

THE RACING DIVE

Diving of any kind is one of the most dangerous activities at the swimming pool. For this reason, *practice diving only under the supervision of an experienced coach.* Make sure the water is deep—the deeper the better. For racing dives, 6 feet is usually sufficient. In pool racing, the start is critical and often determines the winner, especially in sprint races.

For many years it was thought that the best racing dive was when a swimmer dove out almost completely horizontal. However, about 20 years ago swimmers realized that they could go farther out by going higher in the air and deeper into the water. Upon entry, they "scoop" forward and come up farther ahead than a conventional diver would.

The scoop dive entails three basic movements: takeoff, entry, and extension (scoop) (see Figure 5.5).

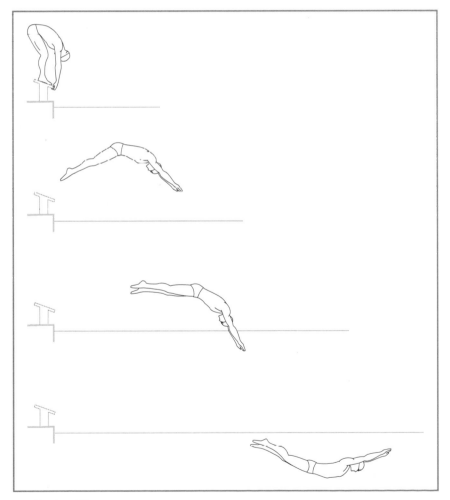

5.5 Racing Dive

Takeoff. Curl your toes over the end of the block, bend at the waist, and hold steady; on the start signal, spring up and out.

Entry. The objective of the entry is to have your hands and feet pierce the same imaginary hole in the water. This means using a slightly piked position.

Extension (scoop). The objective of the scoop is to translate your stored energy (coiled-up body position) into a forward thrust. As you enter the water, straighten out (extend) your body, and be as streamlined as possible. From here, simply glide, kick, and start swimming as you do after a push-off.

With some very solid technique in place, let's turn our focus to training, the workouts and sets that will lock in improvement.

6 Pool Training

Although many find open-water swimming more exciting or interesting, nothing can take the place of a pool for training, for two main reasons:

- The pool is quantifiable—each length is exactly the same, so a 500-meter or -yard in a pool this week is the same as any other week. This precision allows you to track your improvement accurately.
- There are no wind chop, waves, or currents to throw off your technique, especially while doing technique drills.

Doing an open-water swim workout once or twice a week is fine, as long as the bulk (more than 50 percent) of your training is in the pool. Most of your drills and all of your time trials should be done in the pool. In addition, the pool lends itself to interval training, in which you do a set distance a number of times with a predetermined amount of rest or on a specific time interval. Swim training is best done by intervals to help you keep your speed up and pay attention to your technique. The open water lends itself to long straight swims, and doing interval training in open water, though possible, is more difficult.

Are you one of the many swimmers who repeat the same swim training each session year in and year out? Nothing is more common than the fitness swimmer or triathlete who asks, "I swim a mile three times a week, and I am not getting any faster. Why?" Here are the main reasons:

- No focused technique means entropy will take over (see Chapter 3).
- Long slow swims make you a slow swimmer.
- The body adapts to changes in stress: Once the body gets used to a set workout, it stops adapting and actually will start to decrease efficiency.

The third reason is the reason interval training is so important: adaptation from changing stresses. In sports like running and cycling, you can vary the stresses by training on different courses, hills, flats, sand, trails, and so forth. In swimming, you need to make this variation come solely from your effort since there are no "hills" in the water.

Before we get into the nuts and bolts of pool training sessions, let's review some language used to describe pool training in general and interval training specifically.

TERMINOLOGY

Like any other sport, swimming, especially in a pool, has its own language. Knowing these terms won't make you a faster swimmer but will certainly give you more confidence and help you understand the recommendations of a coach if you train in an organized swim practice or follow a workout in a magazine.

Technique drills have been explained in Chapter 3; we are ready to learn how to integrate warm-up, technique work, and main sets to create a robust training program for you. I will define most of the terminology here so that you can become familiar with it and understand the suggested sets better.

Warm-up. This is the time to get used to the water, elevate the heart rate, work on your breathing, and make any goggle/cap/suit adjustments. Avoid the temptation to go fast or work on your technique.

Drills. This is the most important part of your workout. Never, I repeat, never skip this part. This is the time to focus on your technique with laserlike precision. Avoid the habit of simply performing the drills; you need to visualize the drills before you push off, each time. Typically, drills are done as a set of 50-meter/yard swims, changing drills as described in Chapter 3.

Cool-down. As the name implies, this phase is when you cool down after your workout. Cool-down is especially important when you perform a hard main set and need to allow the lactic acid to dissipate from your muscles. Many times after a hard main set, your breathing becomes shortened; the cool-down is the perfect time to get back to a smooth breathing rhythm. It is also a good time to do a few drills to finish practice with good technique so that your body's muscle memory is set to efficient technique.

Set. A group of swims repeated a defined number of times.

Main set(s). This "work" portion of your training session will vary greatly. It is the key set, where a training effect is elicited by the prescribed effort, versus a drill set, where the focus is the technique, not the effort.

Interval. A distance that will be repeated or is part of a progression used in a set. Intervals are often referred to as repeats.

Interval time based. If given an interval time-based set, you leave to start the next interval in the set on that interval time. With this type of interval, your rest depends on how fast or slow your time is on each interval. The faster you go, the longer your rest will be, since you are given the allocated time to complete both the swim and your rest.

Rest time based. If given a rest time-based set, you would rest the allotted time after finishing each interval. No matter how fast or slow you swim, the rest time is the same.

Example: Ten times of a 100-meter freestyle on 1 minute, 30 seconds would be written more simply as 10 × 100 on 1:30, where 10 is the interval or repeat number, 100 is the distance of each interval or repeat, and 1:30 is the interval time. Every 1 minute, 30 seconds, you will push off for the next 100 repeat—this is interval based. If the set had been time based, say for a 15-second rest, then after each 100 swim, you would take 15 seconds of rest, regardless of your swim time.

The following terms help define how a set is performed:

Descending. When each swim in a set gets faster, the times descend with progressive sets.

Ascending. When each swim gets slower, the times for each set will ascend.

Negative split. When the second half of a swim is faster than the first half.

Building. When you start a set and/or swim easy and build speed as you go.

Ladder. A set where the distance goes up and/or down incrementally with each interval.

Base time. A way of giving an interval time-based set for varying distances by giving the swimmer a base time for 100 meters/yards. The swimmer then uses this base to calculate the interval.

Example: Here is a ladder main set: 100-200-300-400-300-200-100 on a 1:30 base, which means the 100 is on 1:30, the 200 on 3:00, 300 on 4:30, and so on. The same set can be given with a rest time of, say, 20 seconds after each swim. If the athlete's pace is well defined, a base time is better; if not, the rest time allows for more flexibility in setting up a program.

Easy speed. When you go fast without pushing all-out or sprinting. This is more subjective "feeling" than an estimated percentage of effort.

Sprinting. All-out fast swimming.

Distance per stroke. Focusing on long, efficient strokes and getting the most distance from each stroke or pull.

THE PACE CLOCK

A valuable tool for managing your workout, especially your main sets, is a pace clock. This is a large clock with a sweep second hand and a minute hand. Generally, the second hand is red and the minute hand is black. It differs from a standard clock in that there is no hour hand, and the numbers go from 5 to 60 in 5-second (minute) increments. The 60 is where the 12 is and the 5 is where the 1 is on a conventional clock (see Figure 6.1).

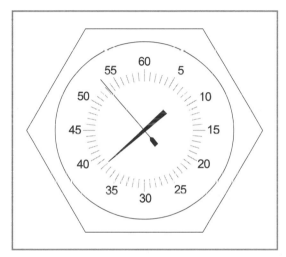

6.1 Pace Clock

Most pools have a pace clock. Learning how to use it can make your workout more effective and easier than operating a wristwatch and trying to read those little numbers with goggles on.

Use of the pace clock is easy. You usually start a set or swim "on the top," or when the second hand is on the 60. If the interval is long, you will need to take note of where the minute hand is so when you finish the swim, you know the number of minutes and seconds it took to finish the swim. When performing sets, you simply leave every time interval. For example, 10 × 100s on 1:45 means that you leave every minute and 45 seconds. Let's say you do a 1:26 on the first 100. That means you get 19 seconds' rest and push off on the 45. The next 100 you do a 1:28, which means you came in when the second hand was on the 13, and you then would get 17 seconds of rest and leave on the 30. The next interval you leave on the 15, then the 60 (on the top), and so on.

The first time you use a pace clock may be a little confusing, but soon you will be proficient and able to use it to help manage your workout.

POOL ETIQUETTE

In addition to terminology and use of the pace clock, there are a few unique and basic rules to follow in the pool for maximum enjoyment—and avoiding a head-on collision. In any pool where there are more than two people in a lane, you will need to *circle swim*. In other words, you always swim on the right side of the lane. This way swimmers will not run into each other, and as long as the speeds are not very different, several people can swim in a lane at one time. See Figure 6.2 to see how this works.

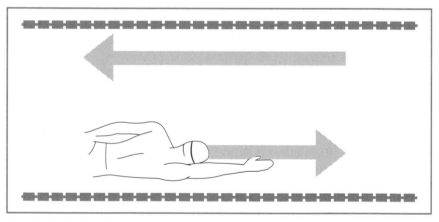

6.2 Circle Swimming

Another point for courtesy is when you want to pass someone. The proper way to do it is to gently tap the person's feet as you approach the wall; then the person stops and lets you, the faster swimmer, pass. Always allow a few seconds after the swimmer pushes off so you do not get right on his feet. If another swimmer is right behind that person, swimming faster than you, it is best to let her go as well.

WORKOUT STRUCTURE

Here is a template that every swim training session should follow. In addition, each of these four parts has a focus that gives the best results:

1. **Warm-up:** Generally 300 to 500 yards/meters; focus on breathing efficiently.
2. **Drills:** 300 to 1,000 yards/meters (see Chapter 3 for details); focus on technique.
3. **Main set(s):** Varies greatly depending on goals and ability level; focus on effort (see below).
4. **Cool-down:** Generally 300 to 500 yards/meters; focus on breathing and technique.

Main Set Recommendations

Do three types of main sets a week: a short interval or speed day (25s, 50s, and/or 100s), longer intervals (100s, 200s, and 300s), and even longer intervals (500 to 1,000). Make most of your sets descending, so you are building speed as you work your way through the set. This approach allows you to maintain good form and your body to adapt to the increase in intensity. If you feel your technique slipping in a main set, don't be afraid to toss a catch-up or fist drill in the middle of the set to "tune up" your technique.

The main sets discussed here are the sets that I have found most effective with our swimmers at every level. These sets demonstrate a starting point for you. They can all be adjusted up or down in distance, with repeat times changed and distances altered and even mixed and matched. Be creative—use these as a framework to create your own personal training program. If swimming with an organized group, you will pretty much need to follow what the coach picks for you. However, many coaches take main set suggestions from the swimmers, and if you are swimming with a group of buddies, you can offer to make the main sets, and then using these proven sets will be very effective. Remember, always do focused and specific technique work—it is more important than training hard!

Interval (Repeat) Times and Rest between Swims

One of the trickiest things in creating effective main sets is picking a repeat time or choosing the rest time between swims in a set. When you do any set, you have the choice of an interval (base) time or rest time between swims. Here are some general guidelines to help you.

In general, you should have shorter rest times in the beginning and middle of your season and longer rest times toward the end. What this approach does is emphasize the aerobic/endurance system by swimming a little slower and keeping the heart rate fairly high in the whole set in the beginning and middle of your season. Then, when the aerobic system is well trained, you swim faster and get more recovery with the longer rest.

Defining Your Effort

You can monitor your effort in many ways, such as using a heart rate monitor, measuring blood lactate levels, and evaluating perceived effort (PE). Perceived effort is not only very effective but the most convenient and least intrusive method to gauge your efforts. Often, coaches and swimmers talk about swims in terms of percentage of a maximum all-out effort. "Race pace" is usually thought to be about 85 to 90 percent PE; this refers to a race pace for a distance swim of 500 to 3,000 meters/yards. An all-out sprint of a short distance (100 meters/yards or less) would be 100 percent PE.

Unlike in running and cycling, the risks of swimming too hard are less crucial, for several reasons:

- The hydrostatic pressure of the water helps flush lactic acid and enhance muscle recovery.
- The cooling effect of the water allows for harder efforts as well as a lower heart rate since the heart does not need to pump blood for cooling the body.
- The horizontal position of the body allows the heart to work a little easier because it is not pumping against gravity.
- Damage to muscles is minimal, especially as compared with running, in which the pounding takes a toll on muscles, joints, and tendons.

Elite-level or pure (swimming the main sport they do) swimmers typically swim two sessions a day, and one is generally very hard.

Imagine running twice a day with one workout a day on the track. The bottom line is, go ahead and train hard in the pool—your body can handle it.

A Word about Easy and Fast

I find it most productive to think about swimming in terms of easy, fast, and various percentages of perceived effort. Avoid the word *slow* to describe any swimming. While the difference between *slow* and *easy* may seem like semantics, your mind certainly hears and feels a difference. Swimming easy is fine (warm-up/cool-down and rest between hard sets, etc.), but swimming slow is not recommended. *Slow* has a negative connotation.

In terms of effort levels and training or energy zones in swimming, the vast majority of swimmers find that using a PE percentage of an all-out 100 percent effort works best. Using any device to monitor heart rate, power, and lactic acid production is not only extremely difficult, but if you could do it, getting the information while swimming is another big challenge. For example, a heart rate monitor while swimming is difficult to keep in place; the bigger obstacle, however, is the fact that you can only read the values when you stop. This does not allow you to adjust your effort as you swim. In addition, the heart rate generally goes up and then drops again when you stop.

So, considering these two issues, it makes sense to work with your own intuitive feeling of what level effort you are putting into the swim. This exercise helps you learn to get in touch with your body's signals and not rely on outside feedback. Here are a few categories of PE:

Easy: Anything under a 65 percent PE, used for warming up and recovering

Easy aerobic (EA): 65 to 75% PE

Fast aerobic (FA): 75 to 85% PE

Threshold (THR): 85 to 90% PE

Anaerobic (AA): 90 to 100% PE

Creatine phosphagen (CP), superspeed: 100%-plus PE

In theory, there is no such thing as 100 percent–plus. The reason I have written it this way is that I have found it best to have athletes assess their percentage of an all-out 100 percent effort for about 1 minute. In swimming, this effort and time duration are equivalent to somewhere between a 75- and 100-meter/yard swim for most athletes. This concept seems pretty easy for most swimmers to grasp once they do a 100-meter race or time trial with an all-out effort.

The last level listed here is for very short durations—so short, in fact, that you will actually not even activate the anaerobic system. You activate the creatine phosphagen system, and you stimulate this system by very short durations of less than 10 seconds. The pace is much faster than you could hold for a minute; hence, I refer to it as 100 percent–plus.

If you were to read several books on exercise physiology and swim training, you could very easily get several definitions of energy systems. Usually the various definitions have many similarities, especially in the recommendation that the bulk of your training be in the aerobic zone (EA and FA). The system that I've offered will define my main set suggestions, because in my 20 years of coaching, I have found this system to be the most practical and effective. For reference, technique drills should be in the easy to easy aerobic zones.

Sample Main Sets

Remember to adjust the number of intervals and amount of rest time as needed. All sets cited here are without units—they refer to either meters or yards.

Shorter Intervals to Work on Aerobic Speed and Power

10 x 100/50. This is a great set to do the 100s at a steady, fast pace, EA or FA, and then make the 50s in between the 100s a little faster, THR or AA. This set is good to do on a rest period as opposed to a time interval, since alternating between 100s and 50s can make following the clock confusing. Do this set with 15 seconds' rest at the beginning of the season and up to 30 seconds' rest toward the end. Also, you can use 25s in place of 50s to really get the speed up.

12 x 50s. This is a great set by itself or as a warm-up set to another longer main set. I generally have athletes descend these in groups of three: first 50 at EA, second 50 at FA, and third 50 at THR. This sequence is then repeated four times. This is a good set to do on an interval time, since as you descend the three 50s, you get more rest.

20 x 25s. This set is another great stand-alone set or can be used as a lead-in to a longer set. Again, I like descending in groups of three or four as with the prior set of 50s. This is a great set to get your stroke rate up.

Longer Intervals to Work on Aerobic Endurance

6 x 200s. The 200 distance makes a great bridge between speed and endurance. Negative splitting is great to do on a set of 200s. The negative splits could be any combination of efforts. My own favorite in the winter is to do the first 100 at EA and the second at FA. As the season progresses and I get more fit, I like to do the first 100 FA and the second 100 between THR and AA pace. The 200s are good sets for throwing in some off strokes for variety—how about an IM? I like four 200s freestyle negative split followed by two 200s IM, one easy and one at THR.

5 x 300s. Sets of 300s are nice to alternate between fast and easy swims. You could swim repeats 1, 3, and 5 at FA and numbers 2 and 4 at EA.

3 x 500s. My favorite way to do these sets is to descend them: EA, FA, and THR. Triathletes should throw in a fast first 200 at the beginning of the last 500 to simulate the beginning of the swim in a triathlon. This strategy helps get them ready to deal with the discomfort of starting off very fast and then settling into an aerobic pace. Due to the nature of a start with many swimmers and the excitement of a race, invariably it is impossible to stay aerobic at the beginning of an event.

Ladder: 100-200-300-400-300-200-100. Ladders are a bridge between short and medium-length intervals. They are great sets for breaking up monotony and forcing the body to adapt to changing distances and pace. A nice way to do these ladders is either to alternate easy and fast swims or to make the swims on the way "down" the ladder faster than on the way "up" (i.e., a negative split ladder). Be creative with the distances. Rest times are better than interval times here since the varying distances make keeping track of the intervals challenging. Again, in early and midseason, go for shorter rest and a little lower intensity (EA and FA); later in the season, go for longer rest and higher intensity (FA and THR/AA).

Very Long Intervals and Straight Swimming

3 x 700. The distance here could be anything from a 600 to a 900. The most important thing in these longer sets is not to get lulled into swimming slow. Pick a certain distance at, say, every fourth length, and make that a "building" length, perhaps going from EA to AA. This makes a huge difference on your pace and body position.

2 x 1,000. Are you aspiring to compete in a long open-water swim or an Ironman triathlon? A set like this one, working up to a set of $4 \times 1,000$, will prepare you better than a straight swim of 4,000. You can vary the speeds on the 1,000s and even toss in a few fast 50s between them for speed. Rest should be 30 to 60 seconds between each set.

Straight Long Swims

They can vary in distance from 500 to 5,000 depending on your fitness, ability, and goals. These swims are helpful in building confidence and endurance; however, you should not do more than one a week or every two weeks since they can lull you into slow and sloppy swimming. Always toss in some pickups during any longer swim and a length or two of technique work to get the most from these swims.

Sample Week

Monday's main set is 10×100s with 20 seconds' rest, all at FA.

Wednesday's main set is 6×200s with 25 seconds' rest, 1 to 4 negative split, EA/THR, 5 easy IM, and 6 an IM at THR.

Friday's main set is $2 \times 1,000$ with 30 seconds' rest, negative split, each one EA/FA.

Note: Each workout consists of a 400 warm-up, 10×50s technique drill, the main set, and a 400 cool-down.

POOL TOYS: TOOLS OR "CRUTCHES"?

Gadgets. Admit it—we all love them. Training can be boring at times, and focusing on some new equipment or device may just give you the diversion you need to get started again. Some gadgets are helpful tools, such as a heart rate monitor for running and biking, and some are just a waste of time and money. Does anyone remember the cell phone holder for the bike?

Essential Swim Equipment

I have scoured the equipment available for swimmers; here is a summary of what I found.

Swimsuit

Yes, of course, you need a swimsuit, but what I want to suggest is that you wear a fairly tight-fitting suit, often referred to as a racing suit. The problem with loose-fitting swimsuits is that they do not allow the swimmer to be aware of the water around the hips and upper legs, which is important for your rotation.

Cap

It is important to keep your hair from distracting your focus from technique. A cap will also protect your hair to some extent from the ravages of chlorine, salt, and sun. Latex caps are inexpensive and can last a while if taken care of. It is best to rinse your swim cap with cool water and dry it after each swim. A little talc or baby powder put in the cap (after it is dry) will keep it from getting sticky and hard to put on for your next swim. Silicone caps are easier to care for and put on/take off; however, they are several times the cost of a latex cap.

Goggles

Although you could swim "naked eyed," a well-fitting pair of goggles will help you see better and save your eyes from the burning and stinging of chlorine or saltwater. Goggles are all about fit. Do not be swayed into thinking that the more expensive a goggle is, the better it will fit. Everyone's eyes are shaped slightly differently, and finding a design that matches your face is paramount. The challenge is that once you buy and use the goggles, they can no longer be returned. My suggestion is to start out with inexpensive goggles or, better yet, try several pairs at the local pool if other swimmers are amenable to allowing you to try theirs. When you find a pair that fits, buy two or three so that you have them if the company changes styles.

Fins

Fins are essential because they are needed for practicing drills properly. The extra propulsion gives you a good body position during the drills. In addition, the fins help with making you more aware of your feet and legs, which helps you keep them in the slipstream of your body and not kick too big or too wide. If you can have only one piece of equipment in addition to a swimsuit and goggles, make it a pair of fins. The fins need to have a short blade so that they give you a little thrust, but not so much that you develop a large kick (out of the slipstream). Zoomers are the ideal short training fin due to their blade length and design, which allow for a natural efficient kick (see Figure 6.3).

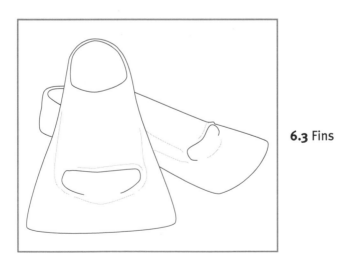

6.3 Fins

The following three items, collectively known as the "swimmer's toolkit," have been staples with competitive swimmers for years, and it is time all swimmers make use of them:

The Tempo Trainer (Swimmer's Metronome)

This device can be set to virtually any stroke rate you desire. You then pop the trainer (the size of a silver dollar; see Figure 6.4) under your cap and start swimming. The trainer beeps at the interval you set. This device is very helpful in maintaining stroke rate during long sets, where strokes tend to slow down and shorten. It is also terrific to use in open water to maintain stroke rate and estimate your distance swum.

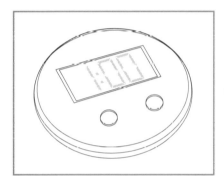

6.4 Tempo Trainer

The Front-Mount Snorkel

Swim coaches have made amazing claims about this product: that it increases breathing capacity and VO_2max (Figure 6.5). What I like best about the front-mount snorkel is that it allows you to take the focus off your breathing (the mechanics of breathing). Not worrying about the timing of the breathing helps many swimmers relax. Moreover, with no movement of the head needed for breathing, you can look at your pull while you swim! One lap with the snorkel, and you will never go back to working out without it again.

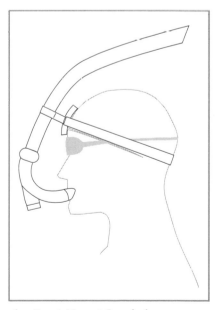

6.5 Front-Mount Snorkel

The Streamliner Hand Paddle

This is the only paddle I use, due to its unique design in size and shape (see Figure 6.6). It actually helps correct your entry and pull. The biggest problem with paddles is that swimmers generally use big paddles with a poor stroke technique, and the extra stress on the shoulder joint can lead to tendonitis ("swimmer's shoulder"). The solution is three-fold: First, check to see whether your arms cross over the midline on both entry and pull. Second, use only a paddle like the Streamliner that places less stress on the shoulder and helps correct poor entry and pull. Third, limit paddle use to 10 percent of your workout distance.

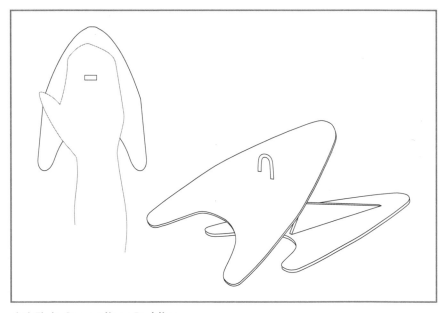

6.6 Finis Streamliner Paddles

Tether

A tether allows you to swim in place. It is basically a belt attached to a stretch cord that is fastened outside the pool. You simply start to swim. Tethered swimming is similar to running on a treadmill. Although this is not the best way to swim, because you are not moving through the water, if you only have access to a small pool, it will allow you to do some training.

Crutches or Damaging Swim Toys

Nose Clips

The only valid use for a nose clip in swimming is if you have a severe reaction to chlorine and have found that a nose clip is helpful. There is a skill to develop of maintaining a slight outward nasal pressure when your head is in the water. This helps with drills, flip turns, and swimming with good technique (the one goggle in/one out breathing position). Once the nose clip is used for any length of time, a swimmer becomes dependent on it and will find it very difficult to swim without it.

Some other problems associated with the nose clip: It makes your inhalations limited to what you can inhale through your mouth. You may forget it. And you may lose it or it might fall off.

Kickboards

Kickboards provide unnatural buoyancy and promote a flat kick with no rotation (see Figure 6.7). It is much better to work on your kick with kick-on-side drills. There are, however, a few valid reasons to use kickboards, such as to learn kicking's basic motion for beginners, to work on kicking power for sprinters, to recover from another type of workout (e.g., a hard run), and to provide a social break for swimmers to chat between swim sets or after a warm-up.

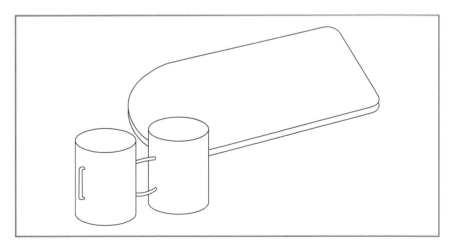

6.7 Pull Buoys and Kickboard

Pull Buoys

These devices go between your legs and float them so that you do not have to kick at all (see Figure 6.7). Lots of swimmers love the pull buoy—why? Because it hides a poor kick and poor or nonexistent rotation. A pull buoy is a lot like a wetsuit: It's a crutch. If you swim faster with pull buoys, guess what? You need more technique work. Trade them in for some fins, and get to work on some kicking, rotation, and body position drills. The only viable reason to use pull buoys is if you have an injured leg; temporarily buoys will allow you to get back to swimming.

Paddles

All paddles I have ever seen (the Streamliner excluded) put added stress on the shoulder and promote a poor pull. Don't risk shoulder injury. Many hard-core swimmers feel that they get a better workout with paddles and pull buoys than with regular swimming. Nothing could be worse for your technique. If you fall into this category, wean yourself from this habit.

Fist Gloves

This is a latex fingerless glove you slip over your fist. If for no other reason than the fact that it looks really weird to have latex wrapped around your fist, you should avoid these gloves. On a technical note, fist drills are most effective when done "dynamically," opening your hands midway through a length so you can feel the added power that a high elbow in the beginning of the pull produces. This movement is obviously not possible with a tight glove on your fist.

PREPARATION FOR OPEN-WATER SWIMMING

Swimming in the pool is the best way to prepare for swimming in the open water. You need first to establish a good foundation on your technique because the added distractions of open water will make it easy to swim sloppily and revert back to old habits. In addition, you can practice the important skill of sighting in the pool so that it is effective when you are in the open water. Even practicing turning around a buoy is good to do in the pool first.

For actually training for open-water races, alter some of the main sets described earlier in this chapter so that you do the first 100 to 300 meters very fast. This strategy is helpful in getting you to simulate the start of a race. Being able to sprint for 2 to 5 minutes and then settle down to an aerobic pace is important.

Now, armed with good technique and fitness from training in the pool, let's venture out to the open water.

7

Open-Water Swimming

WHERE AM I?

What is the most important element of open-water swimming? Navigation, navigation, and navigation.

In a pool, you have the lane lines and painted lines on the bottom of the pool to keep you swimming straight. This experience could lull you into thinking that you swim straight in a pool. No one swims perfectly straight, similar to how an airplane is off course the majority of time and simply corrects often. In the pool, you do not even notice that you are correcting constantly. In open water, the wind, currents, and lack of visibility make swimming without sighting impossible.

Zigzagging around a swim course will have you swimming 4.5K instead of the 3.8K at an Ironman race or perhaps one-third of a mile instead of one-quarter of a mile at the local sprint event. Clearly, more than half of all swimmers do not sight often enough and swim off course. The solution is not to learn how to swim straight, which is impossible due to stroke idiosyncrasies and open-water conditions. The solution is quite simply to sight often. The reason most swimmers do not sight often is that it slows them down and disrupts their stroke. Fair enough, but how about incorporating efficient sighting into breathing?

That approach is exactly what the best open-water swimmers in the world do. Look at the top swimmers in any open-water race, and most are sighting every two strokes or every four. Why? They know that the more often they sight, the straighter they will swim, and they have found a way to sight that does not slow them down. What most swimmers do to sight is simply lift their head and shoulders and swim a few strokes of "water polo stroke" (head-up swimming). While this style is quite effective for seeing where you are going, it makes your legs and lower body sink, shortens your stroke, and increases your effort—all three of which slow you down. The better open-water swimmers incorporate sighting into their regular breathing so the stroke is minimally disrupted.

Few know the importance of swimming straight in open water like ocean lifeguards. To them, swimming straight and keeping their eyes on the victim (swimmer in trouble) can mean life or death. The ocean was my testing ground for developing my sighting techniques. It was not enough for me to be able to swim head-up freestyle; I wanted to be superfast. The thought of getting to the victim one stroke too late was unacceptable and motivated me to learn a method of swimming to maximize both speed and sighting. I innately developed a method to incorporate sighting into my regular stroke so I could maintain my speed and sight simultaneously.

Efficient Sighting Technique

Practice efficient sighting at each swim session in the pool, and soon you will feel more comfortable sighting often, which will translate to straighter swimming and faster times. Here's the method that I developed in my days as an ocean lifeguard.

While swimming normally, start to lift your head from the neck just enough to get the goggles above the water. As soon as you get a glimpse of what's in front of you, immediately continue to rotate to take a breath as you lay your head down on its side. This way you keep your body position level and keep the strokes long by rotating. The challenge here is to time the lifting of your head at the point that your body passes through the flat position (tummy to the bottom of pool or bay). A guideline is to start to lift the head as the opposing arm (to the side you breathe on) is coming forward; as the arm passes your head, turn your head to the opposite side and lay it down on your shoulder (see Figure 7.1). Realize you will probably mess up this sighting technique the first couple of times, but most swimmers get it after only a few practices.

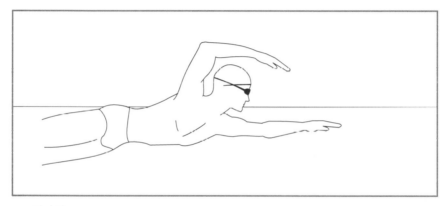

7.1 Sighting

Recommendation: Practicing this sighting technique is best accomplished in the pool first. Until sighting is second nature, add at least one 50-meter/yard sequence of sighting practice to the drills that you do in the technique portion of your swim workout.

DRAFTING

Advantages from drafting exist in most speed sports, including car racing, biking, running, speed skating, cross-country skiing, and, yes, swimming. Percentage effort reduction depends on the sport, and in some sports (e.g., time trialing in cycling), drafting is not allowed. In pool racing, drafting is minimized by the lane lines.

Drafting brings both psychological and physical benefits. Psychologically, you are allowing someone else to carry the burden of leading and not knowing exactly where other competitors are. Physically, the leader is also paving the way, and the water you are swimming in is already moving forward. In cycling, the physical advantage of drafting is estimated at about 30 percent; in swimming, about 10 percent. Of course, this advantage depends on your speed and being in the best possible position (as close as possible without running the person over). Clearly, drafting in an open-water swimming race is a big benefit and is allowed in all types of open-water mass swim events.

Drafting Technique

Like all technique work, drafting is best practiced in a pool without all the distractions of the open water. When circle swimming with lane buddies, you can swim close to them and get "in their draft." Turns in the pool are the challenging part of drafting because each turn breaks up your connection to the swimmer ahead of you, and you need to reestablish it each length.

The main thing is to be as close as possible yet not clawing at the person's feet. When you find someone good to draft off, the last thing you want to do is get him angry by constantly hitting his feet. The optimal position for drafting is directly behind the swimmer. This also allows you to be aware of the other swimmers who may be passing by, and you can get into a faster or slower group as needed.

When drafting, remember to check the following:

- That the swimmer you are following is swimming in the direction you want to go
- That the speed you are going is neither too fast nor too slow for you
- That you do not bother the leader by constantly hitting his feet

SWIMMING IN OPEN WATER

As mentioned earlier when we discussed navigation and efficient sighting technique, open water obviously provides no lane lines to help you swim in a straight line. You should also be aware of other important differences between swimming in open water and swimming in a pool.

Currents, Tides, Wind Chop, and Temperature

Only an outdoor pool with very windy conditions will have any sort of wind chop; most pools are very calm and still. Open water, in contrast, can run the gamut of being flat as a pool to looking like a washing machine and everything in between. Much depends on the type of water you are swimming in, and mostly on the weather conditions.

Because waves, tides, wind, and currents all have an effect on your time, timed swims in open water do not mean as much as they do in a pool. Avoid the temptation to compare times from year to year in the swim portion of a triathlon or an open-water swim event. They will never be exactly the same distance. For swimming, always use pool swims to gauge your fitness, performance, and improvement.

Probably the ocean (versus other bodies of water, such as a lake or river) represents the most potentially challenging open-water conditions, with waves, tides, wind, currents, and water temperature range. What is required for enjoying your open-water training or racing is a healthy respect for the power of water. Conditions in the water can change in a matter of seconds, and keeping a calm head and being prepared can save your life. Therefore, keep in mind the following important safety rules:

- Always swim with a buddy.
- Always swim near a lifeguard.
- Always wear a bright-colored cap.
- Always check the water temperature; do not risk hypothermia.

Spend some time analyzing the area you will be training or racing in. Asking a local swimmer or a lifeguard about the water conditions will usually yield some useful information about the particular conditions to pay attention to. Observing the water for a few minutes yourself also usually gives you most of the information you need. If the water is moving from left to right in front of you, then there is some sort of current or sweep to watch for. Swimming parallel to the shore will be much faster in one direction than in the other. Swimming in and out from shore will be tricky since the sweep will bring you to a different point if you simply line up with where you want to go and try to swim straight.

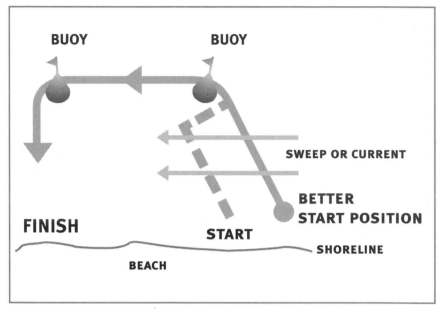

7.2 Handling a Sweep

Figure 7.2 demonstrates this with a current or sweep moving from right to left. In such conditions, a better starting position would be more to the right to take into account that you will be moving to the left as you swim because of the current.

Boats

Like waves, hopefully no boats are in your pool! In most open-water areas, however, boats are a typical part of the scene. Swimming in boating areas is very dangerous, which reinforces the need to swim with a buddy, wear a bright-colored cap, and swim near a lifeguard. The more visible you are, the better chance the operator of a speeding boat or Jet Ski will see you. Although boats are generally not allowed in any swimming areas, having a lifeguard on hand to remind them to stay a safe distance away is helpful and comforting.

Creatures

Okay, so your pool may have some creatures, but most are small and harmless. The open water is another story. Honestly, you have not much more of a chance of getting hurt by a critter in open water than you do in a pool. However, the size of the creatures in the open water can be much bigger, and of course there is the potential (slim as it may be) that a deadly predator will just mess up your day. We all know about the potential danger of a shark attack. Statistics show that the chance of getting bitten by a shark is lower than getting hit by lightning or crashing in a plane. I think the comforting thing should be the fact that only a handful of open-water swimming areas in the world even have the possibility of a shark attack. Again, asking a local or a lifeguard what to look out for is best.

Other creatures that can be annoying are jellyfish. Unless you have an allergic reaction or are bit by a rare poisonous sea animal, jellyfish are more akin to the annoyance of flies on land.

I had a surprise once in a pristine bay that had yet another pesky creature: the aptly named "razor" clam. I stepped on one and got a nice big slice in my heel! The cut took weeks to heal. The lesson: Never assume a nice, calm, pristine open-water area is safe for swimming. Always ask local people whether it is safe and whether you should look out for any particular creatures and conditions.

In most conditions, the most dangerous creatures that you will encounter are humans—the other athletes. My worst swimming injury from a "creature" came in the Ironman® Hawaii in 1993, when another competitor swam across my legs and his (or her?) nail took a 10-centimeter chunk out of my leg! About 2 minutes later, I caught an elbow in my goggle, and the pressure gave me a slice under my eye. Mass starts are brutal. The best protection you can have is to start in an area that is not very dense with competitors. In addition, to protect your head from other swimmers' strokes, re-cover your stroke a little wider. Finally, a good sprint is helpful in getting away from the fray whenever possible.

BUOYANCY

It is a fact: The more buoyant you are, the faster and easier it is to swim. This point refers back to what we said in Chapter 2: Drag slows you down. The less buoyant you are, the more your body is in the water, and the more drag you create. You may have noticed that you feel more buoyant and faster in saltwater. That is because saltwater makes us float better. I have not experienced it, but anyone who has swum in the Dead Sea describes how he or she practically floats on the water. This effect is due to the extremely high salt content of the Dead Sea. Before you get too excited, however, that high salt count can seriously damage your eyes, hair, skin, and swimsuit. Imagine, too, the sting you would experience from a small cut.

I wish that I had the secret of how to make you more buoyant. Short of swallowing air and adding fat (fat floats), there is not much you can do. The more heavy boned a person is, the more that person will sink. The lower percentage of fat someone has, the more that person will sink. In general, women float better than men since on average they are 5 to 10 percent higher in body fat.

More fat may help you float better, but your VO_2max is in direct proportion to your body weight. For most of us, heavier is not healthier, and added weight makes everything you do on land harder. Some of us with the right proportion of fat and light bones will float easier than others. Some "densely" boned athletes with a low percentage of body fat are "sinkers." Not to worry—many sinkers (myself included) can more than make up for their lack of natural buoyancy by improving their technique and getting their body more and more streamlined.

Wait a minute—there is one practical way to increase your buoyancy and reduce your body's drag, instantly.

WETSUITS

Wetsuits have been used in water sports for a long time. They were first made and designed for warmth to allow divers and water sportsmen to stay warm and stay in the water longer. They are called *wetsuits* because they allow water to get trapped between the skin and the neoprene. This water then heats up from your body and provides a warm layer around you. When waters are extremely cold, divers and surfers use a "dry" suit, in which no water gets in. The downside to dry suits is that they restrict motion much more than a wetsuit. When surfers started using wetsuits, the technology improved to allow for increased movement for paddling.

Approximately 10 years after the birth of triathlons, a few athletes started using wetsuits for warmth. They used what was available at the time, suits designed for divers or surfers. They discovered a few things:

- They stayed warm.
- Their strokes were restricted.
- They got chafed.
- They swam faster.

Swam faster? They never expected that result. If anything, they expected to swim slower. Why did they swim faster? They were more buoyant; the wetsuit helped float the body and especially the legs, which made them instantly more streamlined and hence faster. Within a year, companies were making wetsuits specifically for swimming with more flexible rubber and slicker surfaces. The slicker surface made the swimmer faster, again due to decreased drag. It was as though the swimmer's body had been entirely shaved.

How Wetsuits Affect Technique

Although wetsuit technology has improved tremendously and the suits available today are terrific, they will always result in a little restriction in the shoulders, especially the long-sleeved suits. This restriction will shorten your stroke. The key is to make sure you do not fight this effect by trying to force yourself to maintain your stroke length. Instead, allow your stroke to be a little shorter. You will take a few more strokes, but that is fine. The other properties of the wetsuit are so beneficial that this one is negligible, and you do not want to tire yourself out by trying to be an inch longer in stroke length.

Unless you are breaking in a new wetsuit or need it for warmth, avoid using a wetsuit too often because doing so hides technique flaws, especially with the kick. In addition, the suit is most effective when it fits snuggly. The suit stretches with use, so the less frequently you use it, the longer it will last.

Take care of your wetsuit by rinsing it in cool water after each use, drying it both inside and out. Store it in a cool, dry area protected from sharp objects.

OPEN-WATER SWIM TRAINING

Swimming presents more of a challenge for most triathletes than biking and running, for two good reasons. First, you need a good level of technique to swim efficiently in a pool. Second, add the challenges of the open water and many athletes get nervous, even good swimmers.

Entering and Exiting the Water for Competition

Some open-water events start from a beach, others in chest-deep water, and others in deep water. Entering the water from a beach start is challenging, and the best way to do this will depend on the bottom conditions. If the bottom is sandy and gradually gets deeper, then your best method of entering is what is called the "dolphining" method. This is a series of running and shallow dives until the water is deep enough to swim in. Obviously you should never use this method if the bottom is uneven or large rocks appear under the water. Always assess the situation carefully. If the start is from the waist, simply push off and start swimming. When starting in deep water, you will be treading water; simply start swimming when you hear the signal to start.

Exiting the water is more scientific. Many athletes try to stand up way too soon, as soon as they see land. The problem is that if you stand up too soon, you will be in water too deep to start to run. The best approach is to wait until your hand touches the bottom at least three times while swimming. This strategy will ensure that when you stand up, the water will be below your knees and you can run out easily. It will also limit the possibility of cutting your feet on shells, glass, and other debris that may be on the ocean floor.

The Ultimate Open-Water Training Session

Try to do the following session once a week in addition to a few pool workouts, and you will become a well-rounded swimmer. Notice that the only pool drills included are the kick-on-side and the fist drill. The reason is that they are both drills you can do without fins, and one works your body position, whereas the other enhances your pull technique. (Remember which works on what? If not, review Chapter 3.)

Find a safe open-water area with a lifeguard, conveniently close to home or work, and then begin your session:

1. Warm up with easy swimming for 10 minutes.
2. Perform 2 minutes of fist drills and 2 minutes of kick-on-side drills (three strokes to the other side).
3. Do a 4 × 500 set, making each successive rep faster. This set is best done swimming parallel to the shore for 500 meters and then resting there for 30 seconds before coming back 500 meters and repeating. Practice sighting often, and make that sighting as efficient as possible.
4. Practice four entries and exits. Start 25 meters from the water, run in, dolphin three or four times (if the beach area is not conducive to a running start, simply start in chest-deep water), and then swim 25 meters fast. Return toward the shore quickly, and wait until your hands hit the bottom three times; then stand and sprint out of the water to where you started. Take a 30-second rest, and repeat this sequence three more times.
5. Cool down with easy swimming for 10 minutes.

Now that we are back on the shoreline, let's take a look at dry-land training for swimmers.

8 Dry-Land Training for Swimmers

I n addition to whatever workouts and training that specific sports
require, two ancillary training elements are common to all sports
activities: flexibility and strength training. The challenge comes
in adding a doable (from both a time and an energy standpoint)
program to your existing program and lifestyle.

FLEXIBILITY TRAINING (STRETCHING)

Ask most coaches and athletes what they feel they should add to
their program, and many will say flexibility training. In addition,
when we look at an older person and say that she "looks young,"
besides noting the obvious features of hair, skin, and so forth, what
we are really looking at is how flexible the person has remained.
Does he stand erect? Can she bend over to pick up a ball? Can she
twist to see out the side window of a car?

Living makes you tight. That's right—everything we do in the normal course of the day shortens muscles (sitting, driving, working out, stressing, etc.). Maybe this fact is one of the reasons that swimming is such a lifelong sport: It is one of the only sports that elongates the spine as opposed to shortening it.

Although swimming is a sport that in many ways promotes flexibility, improving flexibility in swimming is still important. Swimmers can get many advantages from having flexible shoulders and hips. Flexibility does for swimming what it does for most sports activities: It helps you perform better, reduces the chance of injury, and aids in recovery.

Even with an overwhelming feeling that flexibility training would help them, many athletes find every excuse under the sun to avoid committing to such a program. I think the reason is simple: The gains from flexibility training are subtle and are only seen when you are consistent. This fact can make it an easy part of the program to skip. If we could only view our flexibility training as vital and foundational, then we would make time for it. My suggestion is to commit to a 2-week program and then assess whether the investment of time and energy was worth it.

Many effective methods of flexibility training are possible. Some combine strength work; others do not. Covering all the various methods would be a challenge for an entire book. What I would like to do in this chapter is just share some information on a few methods (in my order of preference). I encourage you to find a method and create a program that you believe in and that fits your schedule. Then, stick with it.

Yoga

The benefits of yoga go beyond adding a little range of motion to your limbs. The breathing is integrated in a dynamic way with the movement, and emotional/spiritual awareness is available to whatever degree you wish to take it to. One of the best aspects of yoga for swimmers, specifically, is its focus on breathing. The improved breathing in terms of fullness and relaxation will have a very positive and direct effect on your swimming.

Yoga comes in many different forms. Ashtanga is considered the "purest" style of yoga and is almost a sport in itself. To be a true "ashtangi," you need to devote 2 to 3 hours a day to practicing it. Many of the same benefits of Ashtanga can be garnered by the more subtle forms of yoga, such as Vinyasa and Anasura. Recently, Bikram, or "hot" yoga, has gained much popularity. This is yoga performed in an overheated (e.g., 104-degree) room. Although the extra sweating under these conditions helps remove toxins, I think it also allows athletes to overstretch their muscles and become dehydrated.

Most yoga studios and health clubs offer a combination of different yoga classes. Take a few and see what you think. (See Appendix C for more information on yoga.)

Active Isolated Stretching

Promoted by Aaron Mattes through his clinics and books, active isolated stretching (AI) is the preferred method of flexibility training for most competitive runners. You can learn a program that will be effective both for warming up muscles preactivity and for recovering and regenerating postactivity. (See the flexibility resources listed in Appendix C for information on Mattes and AI stretching.)

What distinguishes AI stretching from static stretching is the following:

- Activating the opposing muscle to initiate the stretch. A physiological response to a muscle contracting is that the antagonist or opposing muscle relaxes. AI takes advantage of this effect by starting each stretch with an activation of the opposing muscle group.
- Isolating a muscle so that you can see differences between sides of your body. With every stretch in AI, the body is first put into a neutral position to allow stretching of only one muscle or muscle group at a time. For example, the hamstrings are stretched by lying on your back and lifting each leg separately. This technique makes it easy to see any range-of-motion differences between the limbs.
- Holding a stretch for only 2 seconds and doing repetitions. Here is another example of AI taking advantage of muscle physiology. One element in the muscle is called the golgi tendon organ; after 2 seconds of being stretched, this movement tells the muscle to contract, and then a tug-of-war-

type battle is initiated. If the stretch is held long enough, then the muscle gives in and elongates. By holding for only 2 seconds, the muscle never gets into that contraction situation. The muscle is stretched for a total of 16 to 30 seconds depending on how many repetitions are done.

- Increasing blood flow for better warm-up/recovery. By doing repetitions of contractions, the muscles are pumped with blood, which increases heart rate and core temperature— perfect for warming up, preactivity. For postactivity, AI is also great because it will bathe the muscles in fresh blood, flushing out toxins and lactic acid. Many athletes report a feeling after an AI session that is similar to the effects of a massage.
- Increased breathing for toxin removal and relaxation. Breathing is integrated with each stretch. The importance of full breathing for a swimmer cannot be overemphasized.

Static Stretching

I refer to this form of flexibility training as the "stretch and hold" method. This is what most people think about when they think about stretching—for example, lifting a leg on a park bench and bending over to stretch the hamstrings (holding for 15 to 30 or more seconds). While this stretch gets the job done, I feel that it takes a long time and lacks the connection to breathing and mind that yoga and AI offer. Having said that, if you are comfortable with this method and feel it is right for you, have at it!

This type is probably the most commonly practiced form of flexibility training. Ian Jackson's *Stretching* has been in print for decades; it is considered a bible for static stretching (see Appendix A).

Pilates

This method, created by Joseph Pilates, involves work on strength, flexibility, and breathing. The downside is that Pilates can take a good deal of time, and having a good instructor is crucial. I feel that at the end of the day, you are best off with separate strength and flexibility programs.

Nonetheless, many top-level swimmers have incorporated Pilates into their training. One of the leaders in Pilates training specifically for swimming is Dietrich Lawrence (see Appendix C). Dietrich finds that this technique's combination of stretching, strengthening, and focused breathing makes it an ideal part of dry-land swim training.

THE SHOULDER: THE ACHILLES' HEEL OF SWIMMING

Other than shoulder tendonitis from poor technique, tight (weak) shoulders, and/or too fast an increase in training, few swimming injuries typically occur. The shoulder, then, really is the "Achilles' heel" of swimming. You can protect it and decrease any potential problems, however, by keeping the muscles that support the joint limber and strong.

What follows is a short shoulder flexibility program that will help you keep your shoulders loose and increase the range of motion for longer strokes (see Figure 8.1). Aaron Mattes showed this routine to me, and it will only take you a few minutes to do, needs no equipment, and can be done on the pool deck or anywhere.

Shoulder Flexibility Routine

Make sure your form is correct, and, if possible, perform these stretches in front of a mirror.

Note: These exercises (and any flexibility exercises) are to be done without pain. Any pain may indicate an injury and should be treated by a health care professional.

Arm circles (circumduction). Bend at your waist, and swing your arms in opposing circles. Do 10 swings; then switch directions. This is not a stretch but an exercise to warm up (increase blood flow to) the shoulders.

Arms out to side and back (horizontal abduction). Standing straight, bring your arms out and back. Hold at this stretched position for 2 seconds, and repeat 10 times. Bring your arms a little higher and farther back on each repetition. This exercise stretches your chest.

Arms up behind (hyperextension). Standing straight, bring your arms up behind your body. Hold at this stretched position for 2

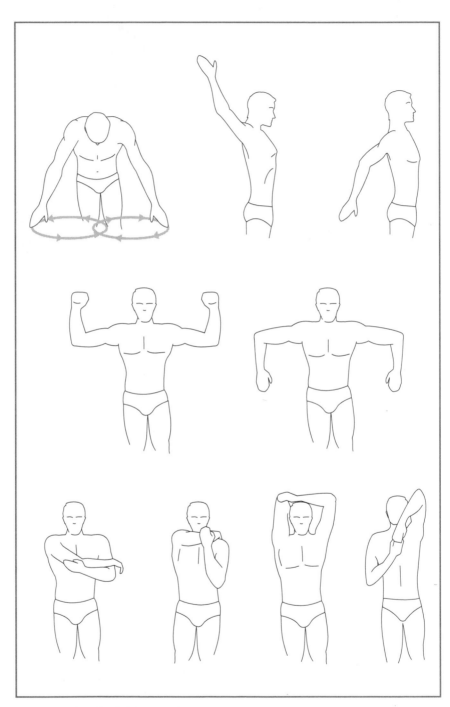

8.1 Shoulder Flexibility

seconds, and repeat 10 times. This move stretches your biceps and the front of your shoulders.

External rotation. Standing straight, lift your arms out to the sides with 90-degree bends in your elbows. Rotate your shoulders backward. Hold at this stretched position for 2 seconds and repeat 10 times. This movement stretches the internal rotators of the shoulders.

Internal rotation. Standing straight, lift your arms out to the sides with 90-degree bends in your elbows. Rotate your shoulders forward. Hold at this stretched position for 2 seconds, and repeat 10 times. This exercise stretches the external rotators of your shoulders.

Arm across chest (horizontal flexion). Standing straight, bring one arm across your body. Assist at the end with your other hand. Hold at this stretched position for 2 seconds, and repeat 10 times. This move stretches your rotator cuff.

Arm across chest, hand over back (horizontal flexion). This is a slight variation on the arm across chest. Standing straight, bring one arm across your body. Drop the hand over your shoulder, and crawl your fingers back. Assist at the end with your other hand. Hold at this stretched position for 2 seconds, and repeat 10 times. This motion stretches your rotator cuff.

Triceps stretch. Although not technically a shoulder stretch, the triceps stretch is important for shoulder flexibility. Standing straight, bring one arm up and back with your elbow bent. Assist at the end with the other hand. Hold at this stretched position for 2 seconds, and repeat 10 times.

Handclasp behind (posterior handclasp). Standing straight, try to clasp your hands in each direction. If you cannot, simply use a rope or a hand towel and inch your hands toward each other. Hold at this stretched position for 2 seconds, and repeat 10 times.

STRENGTH TRAINING

It seems like many athletes are more likely to go to the gym for strength training than to do flexibility training. In their minds, strength is a faster path to improvement. Remember, however, that your power is determined not only by the strength of your muscles but by the range in which they can operate. Also, keep in mind that strength training shortens muscles. This effect makes flexibility training foundational to strength or any other training.

There are two forms of strength training for every sport: sport-specific and conventional (total body strengthening).

Sport-Specific Strength Training for Swimming

As mentioned earlier, the shoulder is the Achilles' heel of swimming. Poor technique, poor flexibility, and lack of strength can add to its vulnerability. Unlike other joints, such as the hip, the shoulder is not held in place completely by its structure. The shoulder (technically, the glenohumeral joint) is reinforced by active muscle support. Four muscles form a musculotendinous cuff around the joint: the supraspinatus, infraspinatus fascia, teres minor, and subscapularis. Because two of these are rotators, these muscles are often referred to as the "rotator cuff." I like to refer to them as the "intrinsic" muscles of the shoulder. When all these muscles are flexible and strong, the joint is well supported. If this area is problematic for you, consult a physician and find a good therapist to work with, one who has had successful experience in working with the shoulder.

Since these muscles are so important for swimming, I suggest you perform the following routine even if you do no other weight training. These intrinsic muscles are small and are trained with light weights; therefore, you do not need a gym. Some athletes start with no weights at all, which is fine because you will increase quickly. Never do these exercises with more than 5 pounds; doing so would recruit other muscles and not engage the small support muscles. You may even use a can of vegetables held in your hand for resistance (start with a 6-ounce can and progress to 12 ounces). Concentrate on your form and breathing. If possible, do these exercises in front of a mirror.

Correct pacing and breathing for this and all strength training are as follows: On the positive movement (lifting or pushing the weight), breathe out. Do this positive movement to a two-count. On the negative (bringing the weights back), breathe in. Do the negative to a four-count. The negative movement is where much of the strength is gained.

Strengthening Routine for the Rotator Cuff (Intrinsic Shoulder Muscles)

The following strengthening routine, combined with the shoulder flexibility routine and good technique, is your best insurance policy for keeping the shoulder strong, flexible, and injury-free:

Lateral raise. Seated or standing, raise your arms out to your sides to shoulder height.

Posterior raise. Seated or standing, raise your arms behind you as high as you can.

Anterior raise. Seated or standing, raise your arms in front of you to shoulder height.

Internal rotators. Lying on your side and using your bottom arm (bent at 90 degrees), rotate your shoulder internally (bring your hand to your chest). Flip to the other side, and repeat with your other shoulder.

External rotators. Lying on your side and using your top arm (bent at 90 degrees), rotate your shoulder externally (bring your hand away from your body). Flip to the other side, and repeat with your other shoulder.

Shoulder shrug. Seated or standing, shrug your shoulders forward in a circular motion. Repeat the shrug movement in reverse.

These exercises can be done while watching TV or conversing with family. No excuses. I have seen way too many swimmers needlessly sidelined because they neglected these muscles.

To increase strength in muscles, you need to work them two to three times per week. Do one to three sets of each exercise and 10 to 15 repetitions. When you can easily achieve 15 reps in good form, it is time to increase the resistance slightly. Remember to do these exercises slowly, working up to 3 pounds. At this point, you only need to do maintenance. No weight increase is needed. As a matter of fact, it would be detrimental because you would stop using the intrinsic muscles and start recruiting larger, surrounding prime mover muscles (these will be worked in the conventional routine, discussed later in this chapter).

Resistance Cords

One of the best uses of your time and energy in strength training for swimming is to use resistance cords or surgical tubing and simulate the pull on dry land. This exercise has a double benefit: It improves technique because you can watch the pull and follow a correct path, and it increases strength following the specificity principle of working the muscles in the same order or pattern that they will be used in your activity. You could spend upward of $1,000 on a "swim bench." The reality is that resistance tubing or even surgical tubing will yield the same, if not better, results, and it is portable.

How to do it: The technique is fairly simple: Attach your resistance tubing to something fixed, bend at the waist, and reach your arms forward. With both arms outstretched, work the elbow bend and pull. The most important part here is the early elbow bend at the beginning of the stroke. To save time, work both arms together. After each pull, slowly take the arms back to the starting position, retracing the movement of the arms backward. Take your time and focus on technique. You can start with three sets of 10 and work up to three sets of 100.

Suggested Strength Training for Swimmers

First, begin with a complete stretching routine of your choice, as described earlier in this chapter, but do include the Aaron Mattes shoulder-stretching routine provided here. Second, strengthen your intrinsic shoulder muscles by completing the rotator cuff routine. Third, for specificity training, do both the resistance cords routine and the shoulder-strengthening routine that I've described. Finally, the total body-strengthening routine described in the next section can be done at a gym with free weights and/or machines. If you are unfamiliar with weight training, have a personal trainer or physical therapist guide you through a workout.

Conventional Strength Training

As mentioned, to increase strength in muscles, you need to work them two to three times per week. Do one to three sets of each exercise listed here with 10 to 15 repetitions each. When you can easily achieve 15 reps in good form, it is time to increase resistance by 5 to 10 percent. For exercises like push-ups that use your own weight, simply keep increasing reps in good form.

1. Squats
2. Leg extensions
3. Leg curls
4. Calf raises
5. Lat pull-downs
6. Push-ups
7. Dips
8. Pull-ups
9. Shoulder press
10. Biceps curls
11. Triceps extension
12. Crunches
13. Reverse sit-ups
14. Back hyperextensions
15. Trunk twists

As in swimming, technique is the most important part of strength training. It does not matter how much weight you lift if you are doing so by jerking it or using momentum and other muscles. Other important notes:

- If you must skip anything in your workout, make it the strength portion, not the flexibility part (stretching).
- If you have only a little time to devote to strength training, do the shoulder- and swim-specific training, and skip the conventional routine until you have more time.
- When performing the conventional routine, try to use free weights as much as possible and do limbs separately. This approach helps you work your balance and frees your range of motion without getting compensation from your stronger side.

- Keep a log, and alternate hard and easy days (periodization).
- A great way to get started with the conventional routine is to join a well-equipped gym or fitness studio and have a session or two with a trainer to get familiar with the equipment. All the other forms of flexibility and strength training do not require a special facility (unless you perform Pilates on a Pilates machine rather than a mat workout at home) and can be done anyplace.

Now, with all the preventative, sport-specific, and total-body flexibility and strength training in place, let's put it all together.

C H A P T E R

9

The Finishing Touches

The technique drills, along with the training information in this book, can be used to form the basis of a solid swimming program for lifelong improvement. Although the topics covered in this chapter are not standard parts of a training program, my experience indicates they can make or break your success.

VISUALIZATION

The power of visualization should always be used. We forget that we have this ability at our disposal at any time. Is it not amazing that at any moment you can decrease your heart rate simply by thinking soothing thoughts?

Use the technique of visualization (seeing in your mind's eye) for both your training and any competitions. Before pushing off the wall to do a swim drill, go through the drill in your mind first, and see yourself doing it correctly. Then push off and do it. The same idea is helpful before an event. See your performance through from beginning to end, even with some potential problems. In your visualization, solve the problems calmly and swiftly. I once was visualizing a portion of a bike race, and in the visualization I got a flat. It made me realize I had forgotten my spare! Try it; play with it; have fun with it.

HAVE FUN

One of the greatest triathletes from the past 20 years and a five-time Ironman® Europe champion, Jurgen Zack, gives this advice: "Training should be fun. If it is not, something is wrong—make a change." This from a guy who does a weekly 120-mile bike ride followed by a fast run! The point is clear: If you enjoy something, you will want to do more of it. See experiences as challenges, not problems.

TIME MANAGEMENT

Make sure your training program fits your lifestyle, or there will be trouble sooner or later. Don't steal from Peter to pay Paul. Maybe you need to skip a running workout to make a yoga class; maybe you need to skip a swim session to do a social activity. Maybe you can combine two workouts and save the time of changing twice or traveling to two places to work out. Remember that "the Beauty is in the Balance."

In Long Island, New York, we have a local training group with a swim session at 6:30 on Tuesday mornings. A group of the athletes will get in a quick run directly after swimming so that by the time they get to work, they have completed two workouts. Remember that the time of day we have best control over is the morning. Once the day gets under way, any number of things can come up to derail our workout plans.

HOW SWIM TRAINING DIFFERS FROM BIKE AND RUN TRAINING

Although we covered this distinction in the chapter on training, it is such a common problem among triathletes that it is worth repeating. Swim training should be technique and interval based. All the details you need are right here in this book. For programs on bike and run training, consult a copy of Joe Friel's *The Triathlete's Training Bible*, one of the other books in this series, or any number of other well-written books on those sports.

REST AND RECOVERY

You improve from a hard workout only when you rest. That is just a physiological fact; however, we think that the workout made us improve. The point is, the training is only as effective as your recovery.

One of the challenges athletes face is that they ramp up their training but fail to increase their rest equally. The result can be an injury, illness, or burnout. If you are upping your training time and effort, be sure you make enough time for rest and recovery.

Rest does not necessarily mean sleep, by the way. Rest and recovery are different for different athletes. For some, they entail reading; for others, a movie. In general, seek quality downtime as an integral part of your training program.

TAPER AND SHAVE

These two components have more meaning to a swimmer than to a cyclist or triathlete. The *taper* is when you decrease your training load in anticipation of an event you want to be well rested for. It is very individualized, so you must experiment, trying different things in training before hard workouts, and see what works best for you. For some, a 4-day taper is best; others prefer a week, and others, 2 weeks.

The length of the event and your fitness level also come into play. Remember that you recover very fast from swimming, so your taper for swimming can be shorter than for other sports. A hard swim session a week before a big event will affect you much less than a hard track session a week before.

In addition to the taper, shaving down the whole body (generally everything that is not covered by the swimsuit) can boost your performance even further. In addition to taking off hair, shaving with a razor takes off two layers of skin. But don't worry—we have seven layers, and the first few are dead anyway. The first dive after a shave gives the body an electrifying feeling. Coming from a competitive swimming background, we swimmers "save the shave" for the big swim meets and championships. I loved the ritual of shaving the night before our championship. It was the final step, like icing on a cake. We had done the training, we had done the visualization, we had gotten the rest, we had the fast swimsuits on, and now we were taking off all unnecessary hair. Shaving was a sign of commitment, readiness, and maybe craziness. When we hit the water, our whole bodies tingled, and we felt fast.

How much did the decrease in drag and increase in sensation count? Depends on how hairy you were and on how much that tingling sensation got you psyched. Some swimmers shaved and tapered well; others had little to no improvement. A 2- to 3-second drop per 100 yards was typical for me when I shaved and tapered. That is 30 to 45 seconds in a 1,500-yard swim (add another few seconds for a 1,500-meter swim).

When I switched to triathlons, I was amazed that triathletes shaved their legs all year like cyclists do. Cyclists shave for the following reasons: a better massage, faster healing and less chance of infection after a crash, and reduced wind drag. If that is the case, let's shave the whole body all year! The only caveat I give you is that unless you are really hairy and a massage is too painful without shaving down, why not save the shave for the really big races for an extra boost? Especially if that race is a nonwetsuit swim. Many of the athletes I train have had awesome swims in the Ironman® Hawaii simply from saving the shave for the race and then shaving the whole body.

If your event is a wetsuit swim, the shave will really not have any physical effect on your swim. It may, however, have a positive psychological impact. As I said before, shaving is that ultimate commitment, stating, "I am ready!"

Unless you bike race a lot, the chances of crashing are not so great that you need to shave your legs. Remember, if you shave all the time, there is less benefit gained at a peak event because the skin is desensitized and you have already become used to the feeling of no hair.

Recommendation: When shaving, use electric clippers first so that you do not go through so many razors.

PROS AND CONS OF SWIMMING WITH A GROUP

In general, training with a group is more stimulating and challenging than swimming on your own. The challenge with group swimming, though, is that you are not on your program but on someone else's. If the group's program provides what you need, fantastic; however, often such a program does not. Many masters swim programs include a good technique session and coaches who can spot errors and offer corrections. However, just as common is the program that hammers the heck out of the swimmers and ascribes to the "strongest survive" principle. Stay away from these programs (unless your technique is solid and you do your own technique work)—they will only tear you down and deteriorate your stroke.

Recommendation: Find a group to swim with a few times a week, and do at least one session a week on your own, focusing on the technique work described in this book.

It is my pleasure to share my knowledge and experience with you. Enjoy your swimming and stay healthy.

APPENDIX A

Defining Your Goals

Whatever your goals are, writing them down is an important step toward focusing your training plan and greatly increasing your opportunity for success. As a matter of fact, many studies (including a landmark 20-year study of a graduating class of Harvard University) have shown that a large percentage of the people who accomplish their goals have written them down. Not surprisingly, the study found that this same group of people ultimately became the most successful and happy with their lives.

The reality is that less than 5 percent of the population actually record their goals. Take an hour or so now to write down your goals. Use this section to help you get an idea of how to go about it, but do not wait until you feel inspired. Just start writing. Think big—you can always pull back. Consider the well-known saying: "Shoot for the moon and you will go far, shoot for the next rooftop and you may fall sadly between here and there and be uninspired."

In keeping with my philosophy on swim training, individualize your goals. If you know yourself to be a person who is not inspired by a large goal, but instead prefer to have a very realistic goal, or an easy-to-achieve goal that you might far exceed, set your goals accordingly. In short, set yourself up for success, not failure.

Ultimately, keep in mind this saying about failure: "There is no such thing as failure, only lessons." Not reaching a goal is really irrelevant! Who you become and what you do on the road to the goal are everything. That is the success or "juice" of the goal, not the goal itself. Try your best to fully appreciate this. Once you understand this, you can make your goals realistic and challenging. Go for it with no fear of falling short. As a matter of fact, falling short is great, as long as you gave it your best. That means you are challenging yourself and are part of an elite group of people who live life to the fullest.

TIPS ON SETTING GOALS

Having and setting goals helps maintain motivation and keeps us on track. The best goals are those that are slightly out of reach. You will discover new things about yourself and find a sense of well-being when you achieve a challenging goal. It is essential to set both long-term (a year or more) and short-term (under a year) goals.

Of course, goals can and should be set in all areas of your life: spiritual, financial, health, emotional, and fitness. For our purposes we will focus on sport goals in general and swimming goals specifically.

Setting individual workout, short-term, seasonal, and long-term goals will help focus your training. Once your long-term goals are established, you can work backward, defining the short-term goals that will lead you to your ultimate achievements. For this reason, short-term goals are called markers, or stepping-stones to let you know how you are progressing toward your long-term goal.

In the same way, if you are a competitive athlete, it is helpful to establish A, B, and C races. An A race is a longer-term goal, and the B and C races are short-term goals to prepare you for the A race.

Example:
An athlete has a long-term goal of finishing an Ironman in 10 hours (Ironman distances are a 2.4-mile swim, 112-mile bike, and 26.2-mile run), with the following splits: Swim 1 hour, Bike 5:30, Run 3:30. (See page 137 regarding different goal times.)

Now, we will set up markers to help this athlete find success in the swim segment.

It is safe to say that in order to swim 2.4 miles in 1 hour (3.8 km or 38×100 meters), you will need to hold a steady pace of just under 1:35 per 100 meters. A great marker set or short-term goal is to do a set of 40×100 meters on a 1:40 interval. It would be a good idea to work toward this goal by beginning with a set of 10×100 on a 1:40 interval holding 1:30 or better. If a 1:30 pace causes your effort level to be nearly "all out," then the goal of swimming 2.4 miles in an hour is really a pipe dream until you can swim 100 meters at 1:15 or better. Following is a systematic way to tackle the challenge.

Work on technique and training to get the speed you need. As you do this you will gain endurance and start to tie a few of these 100s together.

Short-Term Goals

1. Masters meet or time trial, 100-meter swim with a goal of 1 hour, 15 minutes, or faster
2. A main workout set of 5×100 on 1:40 with average time under 1:30
3. A main workout set of 10×100 on 1:40 with average time under 1:30
4. A main workout set of 15×100 on 1:40 with average time under 1:30
5. A main workout set of 20×100 on 1:40 with average time under 1:30
6. A main workout set of 25×100 on 1:40 with average time under 1:30
7. A main workout set of 30×100 on 1:40 with average time under 1:30
8. A main workout set of 35×100 on 1:40 with average time under 1:30
9. A main workout set of 40×100 on 1:40 with average time under 1:30
10. Time trial in a pool (preferably long course), 4 km with a goal of 1 hour or faster

Ideally you could perform this as a main set once a week. The whole 10-step progression can be a 10–14–week buildup, depending on whether you take any recovery/regeneration weeks.

Notes

- Long course is best for triathletes since your time is not aided by pushing off the walls as much as in short course.
- Adding 200 meters while maintaining the same goal time is important for a few reasons: It increases confidence since the distance swam is 200 meters more than the distance of the goal (and the race itself), the extra distance makes up for any gains from pushing off the pool wall on the turns, and when you swim in the race you will probably be going a little easier than in the time trial.

Goals of different times can be pursued in the same way. Simply calculate and replace the goal times. For each additional 2:30 over one hour needed to complete a 2.4-mile swim, add approximately 4 seconds per 100 meters. For example: a time of 1 hour, 10 minutes for a 2.4-mile swim equates to a pace of 1:50 per 100 meters. So the sets would be similar, but you would use an interval time of 2:00 and aim to hold 1:50 or better on each. Similarly, you would need to start with the goal of swimming an all-out 100-meter swim in under 1:40.

APPENDIX B

Training Programs

All three of these training programs are templates and assume that you have been swimming two to three times a week for a minimum of two months. The effort levels described in these programs leave room for you to adjust as needed. In general, "easy" refers to less than 75 percent of PE and "fast" is between 75 and 85 percent of PE. Other levels, such as sprint, are described. Don't be afraid to adjust and alter the training programs to make them work for you. They define a nice progression as you work toward your goal.

Note: You should first warm up with 300–500 meters/yards and execute 20 × 50 drills in each session. The next few pages outline the key main sets.

8-WEEK SPRINT COMPETITION/ SPEED WORK SWIM PROGRAM

This program is for masters swimmers who enjoy sprint races (competing in 50-, 100-, and 200-yard/meter events). It is also useful as an off-season program for triathletes looking to improve their speed.

Week 1 Settle in

WORKOUT	MAIN SET	DESCRIPTION
1A	2 × 400	1 easy, 2 faster, 30 sec. rest interval
1B	5 × 200	all negative split, 15 sec. rest interval
1C	12 × 25	alternating sprint and easy, 20 sec. rest interval
	12 × 50	build speed 1–3, 4–6, 7–9, and 10–12, 20 sec. rest interval

Week 2 Build

WORKOUT	MAIN SET	DESCRIPTION
2A	2 × 500	1 easy, 2 faster, 30 sec. rest interval
2B	6 × 200	all negative split, 15 sec. rest interval
2C	12 × 25	alternating sprint and easy, 20 sec. rest interval
	5 × 50/100	50s easy, 100s fast, 20 sec. rest after 50 and 100

Week 3 Build

WORKOUT	MAIN SET	DESCRIPTION
3A	2 × 600	1st 600: alternate 50 easy and 50 fast 2nd 600: negative split, 30 sec. rest interval
3B	6 × 200	build speed 1–3 and 4–6, 15 sec. rest interval
3C	16 × 25	alternate sprint and easy, 20 sec. rest interval
	6 × 50/100	50s fast, 100s easy, 20 sec. rest after 50 and 100

Week 4 Recovery week

WORKOUT	MAIN SET	DESCRIPTION
4A	2 × 400	1 alternate 50 easy and 50 fast, 2 negative split, 30 sec. rest interval
4B	4 × 200	negative split, 20 sec. rest interval
4C	12 × 25	alternate sprint and easy, 20 sec. rest interval
	12 × 50	build speed 1–3, 4–6, 7–9, and 10–12, 20 sec. rest interval

Week 5 Build

WORKOUT	MAIN SET	DESCRIPTION
5A	1,000	negative split
5B	5 × 200	1, 3, and 5 fast; 2 and 4 easy; 30 sec. rest interval
5C	20 × 25	alternate sprint and easy, 20 sec. rest interval
	10 × 100	at threshold, 20 sec. rest interval after each and hold the fastest average time

Week 6 Build

WORKOUT	MAIN SET	DESCRIPTION
6A	1,200	negative split
6B	6 × 200	3 and 6 fast; 1, 2, 4, and 5 easy; 25 sec. rest
6C	12 × 25	half-pool sprints with full recovery, 45–60 sec. rest interval
	10 × 50	all fast with 20 sec. rest interval
	5 × 100	1, 3, and 5 fast; 2 and 4 easy/ 30 sec. rest interval

Week 7 Taper

WORKOUT	MAIN SET	DESCRIPTION
7A	2 × 500	1 easy, 2 fast, 30 sec. rest interval
7B	5 × 200	1st 200: fast 2nd 200: 150 fast/50 easy 3rd 200: 100 fast/100 easy 4th 200: 50 fast/150 easy 5th 200: fast again 30 sec. rest interval
7C	16 × 25	half-pool sprints with full recovery, 45–60 sec. rest interval
	8 × 50	all fast with 20 sec. rest interval
	3 × 100	1 and 3 fast, 2 easy, 45 sec. rest interval

Week 8 Race

WORKOUT	MAIN SET	DESCRIPTION
8A	2 × 300	1 easy, 1 fast, 45 sec. rest interval
8B	5 × 200	1 and 4 easy, 2 and 3 easy, 45 sec. rest interval
8C	RACE	You are ready!

12-WEEK SPRINT OR OLYMPIC TRIATHLON SWIM PROGRAM

This program is for masters swimmers and/or triathletes planning to swim a distance from 400 to 1,500 meters (or approximately 500–1,650 yards), in either a pool race or an open-water race.

Week 1 Settle in

WORKOUT	MAIN SET	DESCRIPTION
1A	2 × 400	1 easy, 2 faster, 30 sec. rest interval
1B	5 × 200	all negative split, 15 sec. rest interval
1C	12 × 25	alternate sprint and easy, 20 sec. rest interval
	12 × 50	build speed 1–3, 4–6, 7–9, and 10–12, 20 sec. rest interval

Week 2 Build

WORKOUT	MAIN SET	DESCRIPTION
2A	1,000	every 4th length pick up speed
2B	6 × 200	all negative split, 15 sec. rest interval
2C	12 × 25	alternate sprint and easy, 20 sec. rest interval
	5 × 50/100	50s easy, 100s fast, 20 sec. rest after 50 and 100

Week 3 Build

Workout	Main Set	Description
3A	2 × 600	1 alternate 50 easy and 50 fast, 2 negative split, 30 sec. rest interval
3B	6 × 200	build speed 1–3 and 4–6, 15 sec. rest interval
3C	16 × 25	alternate sprint and easy, 20 sec. rest interval
	6 × 50/100	50s fast, 100s easy, 20 sec. rest after 50 and 100

Week 4 Recovery/Regeneration

Workout	Main Set	Description
4A	1,500	every 4th length pick up speed
4B	4 × 200	negative split, 20 sec. rest interval
4C	12 × 25	alternate sprint and easy, 20 sec. rest interval
	12 × 50	build speed 1–3, 4–6, 7–9, and 10–12, 20 sec. rest interval

Week 5 Build

Workout	Main Set	Description
5A	3 × 500	descend with 20 sec. rest
5B	5 × 200	1, 3, and 5 fast; 2 and 4 easy; 30 sec. rest interval
5C	20 × 25	alternate sprint and easy, 20 sec. rest interval
	10 × 100	at threshold, 20 sec. rest interval after each and hold the fastest average time

Week 6 Build

Workout	Main Set	Description
6A	1,500	time trial
6B	6 × 200	3 and 6 fast; 1, 2, 4, and 5 easy; 25 sec. rest interval
6C	12 × 25	sprints with full recovery, 45–60 sec. rest interval
	10 × 50	all fast with 20 sec. rest interval
	5 × 100	1, 3, and 5 fast; 2 and 4 easy; 30 sec. rest interval

Week 7 Build

Workout	Main Set	Description
7A	3 × 600	descend with 20 sec. rest
7B	5 × 200	1st 200: fast
		2nd 200: 150 fast/50 easy
		3rd 200: 100 fast/100 easy
		4th 200: 50 fast/150 easy
		5th 200: fast again
		30 sec. rest interval
7C	16 × 25	half-pool sprints with full recovery, 45–60 sec. rest interval
	12 × 100	at threshold, 20 sec. rest interval after each and hold the fastest average time

Week 8 Recovery/Regeneration

Workout	Main Set	Description
8A	2 × 500	1 easy and 1 fast, 30 sec. rest interval
8B	5 × 200	1 and 4 easy, 2 and 3 easy, 45 sec. rest interval
8C	10 × 100	double set of drills, alternate easy and fast with 20 sec. rest interval

Week 9 Build

Workout	Main Set	Description
9A	2,000	time trial
9B	6 × 300	3 and 6 fast; 1, 2, 4, and 5 easy; 25 sec. rest interval
9C	12 × 25	half-pool sprints with full recovery, 45–60 sec. rest
	10 × 50	all fast with 20 sec. rest interval
	5 × 100	1, 3, and 5 fast; 2 and 4 easy; 30 sec. rest interval

Week 10 Speed/Build

Workout	Main Set	Description
10A	3 × 500	descend with 30 sec. rest interval
10B	5 × 300	3 speeds on each 300: 1st 100 easy, 2nd faster, and 3rd superfast, 30 sec. rest interval
10C	18 × 25	half-pool sprints with full recovery, 45–60 sec. rest interval
	15 × 100	at threshold, take 30 sec. rest interval each and hold the fastest average time

Week 11 Taper

Workout	Main Set	Description
11A	1,500	time trial
11B	5 × 200	1, 3, and 5 fast; 2 and 4 easy; 40 sec. rest interval
11C	20 × 25	half-pool sprints with full recovery, 45–60 sec. rest interval
	6 × 100	descend 1–3 and 4–6, 50 sec. rest interval

Week 12 Race

Workout	Main Set	Description
12A	2 × 300	1 easy, 2 alternate fast/easy by 100s, 30 sec. rest interval
12B	8 × 25	half-pool sprints with full recovery, 45–60 sec. rest interval
	5 × 100	1, 3, and 5 fast; 2 and 4 easy; 40 sec. rest interval
12C	RACE	You are ready!

16-WEEK LONG-DISTANCE TRIATHLON SWIM PROGRAM

This program is for masters swimmers and/or triathletes preparing to swim a distance from 1.2 to 2.4 miles (approximately 1,900–3,800 meters).

Week 1 Settle in

WORKOUT	MAIN SET	DESCRIPTION
1A	2 × 400	1 easy, 2 faster, 30 sec. rest interval
1B	5 × 200	all negative split, 15 sec. rest interval
1C	12 × 25	alternate sprint and easy, 20 sec. rest interval
	12 × 50	build speed 1–3, 4–6, 7–9, and 10–12, 20 sec. rest

Week 2 Build

WORKOUT	MAIN SET	DESCRIPTION
2A	1,000	every 4th length pick up speed
2B	6 × 200	all negative split, 15 sec. rest interval
2C	12 × 25	alternate sprint and easy, 20 sec. rest interval
	5 × 50/100	50s easy, 100s fast, 20 sec. rest after 50 and 100

Week 3 Build

Workout	Main Set	Description
3A	2 x 600	1st 600: alternate 50 easy and 50 fast 2nd 600: negative split, 30 sec. rest interval
3B	6 × 200	build speed 1–3 and 4–6, 15 sec. rest interval
3C	16 × 25	alternate sprint and easy, 20 sec. rest interval
	6 × 50/100	50s fast, 100s easy, 20 sec. rest after 50 and 100

Week 4 Recovery/Regeneration

Workout	Main Set	Description
4A	1,500	every 4th length pick up speed
4B	4 × 200	negative split, 20 sec. rest interval
4C	12 × 25	alternate sprint and easy, 20 sec. rest interval
	12 × 50	build speed 1–3, 4–6, 7–9, and 10–12, 20 sec. rest interval

Week 5 Build

Workout	Main Set	Description
5A	3 × 500	descend with 20 sec. rest
5B	5 × 200	1, 3, and 5 fast; 2 and 4 easy; 30 sec. rest interval
5C	20 × 25	alternate sprint and easy, 20 sec. rest interval
	10 × 100	at threshold, 20 sec. rest interval after each and hold the fastest average time

Week 6 Build

WORKOUT	MAIN SET	DESCRIPTION
6A	2,000	time trial
6B	6 × 200	3 and 6 fast; 1, 2, 4, and 5 easy; 25 sec. rest interval
6C	12 × 25	half-pool sprints with full recovery, 45–60 sec. rest interval
	10 × 50	all fast with 20 sec. rest interval
	5 × 100	1, 3, and 5 fast; 2 and 4 easy; 30 sec. rest interval

Week 7 Build

WORKOUT	MAIN SET	DESCRIPTION
7A	3 × 600	descend with 20 sec. rest interval
7B	5 × 200	1st 200: fast 2nd 200: 150 fast/50 easy 3rd 200: 100 fast/100 easy 4th 200: 50 fast/150 easy 5th 200: fast again 30 sec. rest interval
7C	16 × 25	half-pool sprints with full recovery, 45–60 sec. rest interval
	12 × 100	at threshold, 20 sec. rest interval after each and hold the fastest average time

Week 8 Recovery/Regeneration

WORKOUT	MAIN SET	DESCRIPTION
8A	2 × 500	1 easy, 2 fast, 30 sec. rest interval
8B	5 × 200	1 and 4 easy, 2 and 3 easy, 45 sec. rest interval
8C	10 × 100	double set of drills, alternate easy and fast, 20 sec. rest interval

Week 9 Build

WORKOUT	MAIN SET	DESCRIPTION
9A	2,000	time trial
9B	6 × 300	3 and 6 fast; 1, 2, 4, and 5 easy; 25 sec. rest interval
9C	12 × 25	half-pool sprints with full recovery, 45–60 sec. rest interval
	10 × 50	all fast, 20 sec. rest interval
	5 × 100	1, 3, and 5 fast; 2 and 4 easy; 30 sec. rest interval

Week 10 Build

WORKOUT	MAIN SET	DESCRIPTION
10A	4 × 500	negative split with 30 sec. rest interval
10B	8 × 200	descend 1–4 and 5–8, 30 sec. rest interval
10C	18 × 25	half-pool sprints with full recovery, 45–60 sec. rest
	15 × 100	at threshold, 30 sec. rest interval after each and hold the fastest average time

Week 11 Build

WORKOUT	MAIN SET	DESCRIPTION
11A	2,500	every 4th length pick up speed
11B	8 × 300	all negative splits, 25 sec. rest interval
11C	20 × 25	half-pool sprints with full recovery, 45–60 sec. rest interval
	6 × 100	descend 1–3 and 4–6, 50 sec. rest interval

Week 12 Recovery/Regeneration

WORKOUT	MAIN SET	DESCRIPTION
12A	2 × 600	1st 600: easy 2nd 600: alternate fast and easy by 100s, 30 sec. rest interval
12B	5 × 300	3 speeds on each 300 (100 easy, 100 fast, and 100 faster), 30 sec. rest interval
12C	8 × 25	half-pool sprints with full recovery, 45–60 sec. rest interval
	5 × 100	1, 3, and 5 fast; 2 and 4 easy; 40 sec. rest interval

Week 13 Build

WORKOUT	MAIN SET	DESCRIPTION
13A	3,500	time trial
13B	6 × 300/100	300s easy and 100s very fast
13C	20 × 25	half-pool sprints with full recovery, 45–60 sec. rest interval
	20 × 100	at threshold, 30 sec. rest interval after each and hold the fastest average time

Week 14 Build

WORKOUT	MAIN SET	DESCRIPTION
14A	5 × 500	1, 3, and 5 fast; 2 and 4 easy
14B	6 × 300/150	300s fast and 150s easy, 30 sec. rest
14C	20 × 25	half-pool sprints with full recovery, 45–60 sec. rest interval
	25 × 100	at threshold, 30 sec. rest interval after each and hold the fastest average time

Week 15 Taper

Workout	Main Set	Description
15A	4,000	time trial
15B	10 × 200	1–5 descend, 6–10 negative split, 30 sec. rest interval
	10 × 200	1–5 descend, 6–10 negative split, 30 sec. rest interval
15C	20 × 25	half-pool sprints with full recovery, 45–60 sec. rest interval
	10 × 100	1–5 easy, 6–10 race pace (fast but comfortable)

Week 16 Race

Workout	Main Set	Description
16A	2 × 300	1 easy, 2 alternate fast/easy by 100s, 30 sec. rest interval
16B	8 × 25	half-pool sprints with full recovery, 45–60 sec. rest interval
	5 × 100	1, 3, and 5 fast; 2 and 4 easy; 40 sec. rest interval
16C	RACE	You are ready!

APPENDIX C

Additional Resources

FLEXIBILITY TRAINING

Active Isolated Stretching

Aaron Mattes, producer of books, videos, and clinics
PO Box 17217
Sarasota, FL 34276–0217
941-922-1939, 941-927-6121 fax
www.stretchingusa.com

Static Stretching

Bob Anderson
Stretching, Inc.
PO Box 767
Palmer Lake, CO 80133
800-333-1307, 719-481-9058 fax
e-mail: office@stretching.com
www.stretching.com

Pilates

Dietrich Lawrence
The Classic Physique
"Pilates Gym on the Big Island"
74-5583 Pawai Place #B130
Kailu-Kona, HI 96740
808-329-9600

Yoga

Yoga for Endurance Athletes (DVD), a 24-minute routine perfect for swimmers, cyclists, runners, and triathletes, produced in 2005 and available at www. TTUniversity.com.

REFERENCES

Chambliss, Daniel F. *Champions: The Making of Olympic Swimmers*. New York: William Morrow, 1998.
An inside view of Viejo programs.

Counsilman, James. *The Complete Book of Swimming*. New York: Atheneum, 1977.
From the man who brought swimming out of the dark ages with his 1968 book, *The Science of Swimming* (Prentice Hall). "Doc" Counsilman exudes love from swimming in every sentence.

Fahey, Thomas D. *Basic Weight Training for Men & Women*, 2nd ed. Mountain View, CA: Mayfield, 1994.
A good book on working various muscles using free weight machines.

Gallagher, Harry. *Harry Gallagher on Swimming*. London: Pelham, 1970.
The history of swimming and timeless principles from one of Australia's finest coaches.

Maglischo, Ernest W. *Swimming Fastest*. Champaign, IL: Human Kinetics, 2003.

Ryan, Frank. *Backstroke Swimming*. New York: Viking, 1974.

Ryan, Frank. *Breaststroke Swimming*. New York: Viking, 1974.

Ryan, Frank. *Butterfly Swimming*. New York: Viking, 1974.
Three books that are great for beginners.

Whitten, Phillip. *The Complete Book of Swimming*. New York: Random House, 1994.
Has a terrific appendix that includes world age-group and masters records.

ADDITIONAL READING

Balch James, and Phyllis Balch. *Nutritional Healing*. Garden City, NY: Avery, 1990.
Technical questions on nutrition.

Chavoor, Sherman. *The 50-meter Jungle: How Olympic Gold Swimmers Are Made*. Coward, McCann, Geoghegan, 1973.
Behind the scenes of the greatest swimmer of all time, Mark Spitz.

Friel, Joe. *The Triathlete's Training Bible*, 2nd ed. Boulder, CO: VeloPress, 2004.

Haas, Robert. *Eat to Succeed: The Haas Maximum Performance Program*. New York: Rawson Associates, 1986.
Includes good tips on the athlete and nutrition and takes a nice approach to achieving balance in terms of diet.

Haas, Robert. *Eat to Win: The Sports Nutrition Bible*. New York: Rawson Associates, 1983.

Sprawson, Charles. *Haunts of the Black Masseur: The Swimmer as Hero*. New York: Pantheon Books, 1992.
Explores swimming on the ultra-esoteric side.

PUBLICATIONS

Swim, Swimming World, Swimming Technique
PO Box 20337
Sedona, AZ 86341
928-284-4005, 928-284-2477 fax
www.swiminfo.com

Three magazines published for slightly different audiences:

Swimming World is for age-group and national-level competitors, and *Swimming Technique* is for coaches and techies.

Inside Triathlon (magazine)
Inside Communications
1830 North 55th Street
Boulder, CO 80301
303-440-0601, 303-444-6788 fax
www.insidetri.com
An informative triathlon publication with many articles on training.

Triathlete (magazine)
328 Encinitas Boulevard, Suite 100
Encinitas, CA 92024
760-634-4100, 760-634-4110 fax
www.triathletemag.com
A triathlon publication published in the United States, France, and Italy.

SWIMMING ORGANIZATIONS

United States

USA Triathlon
PO Box 15820
Colorado Springs, CO 80935
719-578-4578
www.USAtriathlon.org
The national governing body for triathlons. Some races require membership.

USA Swimming
1750 East Boulder Street
Colorado Springs, CO 80909
719-578-4578
www.usaswimming.org
The national governing body for senior, age-group, and Olympic
swimmers.

United States Masters
2nd Peter Avenue
Rutland, MA 01543
508-886-6631
www.usms.org
The governing body for masters swimming, ages 19 and up.

International

Amateur Swimming Federation of the Great Britain
(includes masters)
Harold Fern House
Derby Square
Loughborough, Leicestershire LE11 5AL
England
01509-518-700

Aussi Masters Swim Inc.
PO Box 207
Cowan Dilla SA5033
Australia
08-3441217
www.aussimasters.com.au

Canada Masters National Office
c/o Jackie Spry
Box 526
Elmsdale, Nova Scotia
Bonimo
902-883-8833
www.mastersswimmingcanada.ca

Index

AA. *See* Anaerobic

Active isolated stretching (AI), 119-20

Aerobic, 3-4, 92, 103

Aerobic endurance (AE), 95-96

Aerobic power, 94-95

Aerobic speed, 94-95

AI. *See* Active isolated stretching

Anaerobic (AA), 68, 69, 77, 92, 93, 94

Anterior raise, 125

Anterior tibialis, 23

Arm cycles, 72

    advanced techniques for, 77-78

    backstroke, 56-57

    breaststroke, 60-61

    butterfly, 64

    freestyle, 24

    phases of, 24-25

Australian crawl. *See* Freestyle

Back bends, 29

Back floating, 56

Back hyperextensions, 127

Backstroke, 55-58, 59

arm cycle for, 56-57

basics of, 54-55

drills for, 57-58

drills for, 57-58

freestyle and, 72

IM and, 54

kick for, 57, 58 (fig.)

open water and, 53, 55

pull for, 58 (fig.)

single-arm, 57-58

technique for, 56-57

Balance, 2, 11, 18, 53, 68, 72, 130

Base time, 88

Biceps curls, 127

Biking, 2, 70, 86, 97, 114, 131

    drafting and, 108

Blood flow, 121

    warm-up/recovery and, 120

Blood lactate levels, 92

Blood volume, 16

Boat lessons, 30

Boats, open water and, 110

Body position, 23, 30, 98

    correct, 20

Body position (cont'd)
   correct, 20
   drills for, 24, 37–40
   fins and, 102
   good, 27
   improving, 19, 25, 54
   streamlining, 20
Bones, dense, 112
Breaststroke, 7, 56, 59–62
   arm cycle for, 60–61
   basics of, 54–55
   butterfly and, 63
   feel for the water and, 54
   IM and, 54
   kick for, 61, 62, 62 (fig.), 63
   legal, 60, 76
   open water and, 53, 59
   pull for, 61, 62, 62 (fig.)
   technique for, 60–61, 62
   wave, 60
Breath control swims, 68–69
Breathing, 2, 7, 8, 12, 20–21, 22
      (fig.), 51, 86, 101, 107
   alternate, 17–19
   bilateral, 16, 17–19
   deeper, 69, 99, 118
   efficient, 21, 69, 125
   exercises for, 16, 18, 19 (fig.)
   flip turns and, 82
   focusing on, 14–19, 68, 91, 121,
      124
   freestyle and, 15, 16
   kicks and, 78
   patterns for, 16–19, 55, 68–69
   relaxation and, 120
   rotation and, 21
   sighting and, 106
   stretching and, 120
   strokes and, 15, 16, 17, 18, 68,
      69, 106
   technique and, 79, 99
   toxin removal and, 120

Building, 88
Buoyancy, 101
   drag and, 111, 112
   salinity and, 13, 111, 112
Buoys, 59
   pull, 101 (fig.), 102
Burnout, rest/recovery and, 131
Butterfly, 53, 56, 59, 60, 63–66, 77
   arm cycle for, 64
   basics of, 54–55
   breaststroke and, 63
   feel for the water and, 54
   IM and, 54
   kick for, 62, 65 (fig.), 66
   pull for, 64, 65 (fig.)
   technique for, 63–64, 66

Calf raises, 127
Caps, 97, 109, 110
Catch-up drill, 41, 41 (fig.), 47, 50,
      51, 79
Catch-up drill with fingertip drag,
      42, 42 (fig.)
Catch-up drill with thumb scrape,
      42, 42 (fig.), 48
Challenges, 6–7, 9, 12–14, 114
Chlorine, 97, 101
Circle swims, 90, 90 (fig.)
Circumduction, 121
Collisions, 70, 90, 132
Cool-downs, 15, 87, 91, 92, 93, 115
Coordination, 53, 78
Core muscles, 23
   strengthening, 29, 63
Core temperature, 120
Corkscrew drill, 38, 38 (fig.)
CP. See Creatine phosphagen
Cramping, treading water and, 14
Crawl. See Freestyle
Creatine phosphagen (CP), 71, 93,
      94
Creatures, open water and, 110–11
Crocker, Ian, 76–77

Crosstraining, 15
Crunches, 127
Crutches, 101-3
Currents, 85, 105, 109-10

Deep-water starts, 12
Dehydration, 119
Descending, 88
Dips, 127
Distance per stroke, 88
Distance swimming, 21, 75
    kick/pull and, 24
    sprint swimming and, 69-71
Dives, 76, 82-84, 83 (fig.)
Dolphining, 76-77, 114, 115
Dolphin kick, 63
Drafting, 70, 107-8
Drag, 7
    buoyancy and, 111, 112
    creating, 47, 50, 57
    reducing, 19, 20, 22, 28, 54, 132
    streamlining and, 55
    wetsuits and, 113
Drills, 24, 87, 91, 114
    backstroke, 57-58
    breaststroke, 62
    butterfly, 66
    combining, 46
    effective, 51
    focusing on, 35, 45
    freestyle, 34, 36-44, 57-58, 66
    tips for, 45-46
Dropping elbow, pressing down
    on pull, 48, 49 (fig.)
Drowning, 9, 14
Dry suits, 112

EA. See Easy aerobic
Early entry, 47-48, 47 (fig.)
Easy:
    fast and, 93-94
    slow and, 93
Easy aerobic (EA), 93, 94

Easy speed, 88
Efficiency, 2, 10, 17, 19-25, 80
    improving, 6, 7, 30, 35, 45
    reducing, 69, 86
Effort, 92-93, 94
    reducing, 106, 107
Elbow bend, 25, 30, 79
    early, 28
    pull and, 55
    working on, 126
Elbow flexion, 56, 61, 64
Elbows, dropping, 28, 48, 49 (fig.)
Endurance system, 92
Energy
    production cycle, 15
    wasting, 22
    zones, 93
Entropy, 33-35, 86
Entry, 24, 56, 64, 79, 83, 84
    correcting, 100
    early, 47-48, 47 (fig.)
    lengthening, 72
    open water, 114, 115
    overextending, 51, 51 (fig.)
    slapping, 51, 51 (fig.)
Equipment, thoughts on, 36,
    97-103
Esselstyn, Rip, 77, 78, 79
Etiquette, 90
Evans, Janet, 31
Exiting open water, 114, 115
Extension, 83, 84
External rotation, 123
External rotators, 125

FA. See Fast aerobic
Fast, easy and, 93-94
Fast aerobic (FA), 93, 94
Fat, buoyancy and, 112
Fear, 8-9, 14
Fingertip drag drill, 48, 51
Fins, 29, 64, 77, 98 (fig.), 114

Fins (cont'd)
  drills with, 36, 45, 66, 98, 102
  Zoomer, 36, 66, 98
Fish-tailing, 23, 47
Fist drill, 36, 44, 44 (fig.), 45, 48,
  114, 115
Fist gloves, 102
Fitness, 3, 30, 109
Flat swimming, 48, 107
Flexibility, 4, 23, 127
  poor, 124
  shoulder, 121, 122 (fig.), 123
  strength programs and, 120
  training, 117–21, 124, 128
Flip turns, 25, 56, 79–82, 81 (fig.)
  breathing and, 82
  flat, 81
  missing, 82
  phases of, 80
Flow state, 54
Flutter, 21–23, 55, 56
Foundation, 45, 67
Freestyle, 1, 21–23, 24, 28, 53, 56,
  59, 61, 63, 64, 77
  backstroke and, 72
  breathing and, 15, 16
  development of, 8, 60
  distance, 69
  drills for, 34, 36–44, 57–58, 66
  efficient, 71
  flaws in, 46–51
  focusing on, 11–14
  head-up, 106
  IM and, 54
  improving, 7, 34, 55, 67
  kicks for, 23, 75
  physics of, 33
  sprint, 69
Free weights, 126
Friel, Joe, 131

Genetics, 28

Gliding, 57–58
Goggles, 55, 97–98, 101

Head:
  position, 50, 50 (fig.), 80
  protecting, 111
  stationary, 57
Heart rate monitors, 92, 93, 97
Heart rates, 16, 92, 120, 129
Horizontal abduction, 121
Horizontal flexion, 123
Horizontal position, 92
Hydrostatic pressure, 92
Hyperextension, 123
Hypothermia, 109

Illnesses, rest/recovery and, 131
IM. See Individual medley
Improvements, 5, 9, 10, 131
  gauging, 85, 109
  maximizing on, 28
Individual medley (IM), 54, 66
Injuries, 118, 121
  rest/recovery and, 131
  shoulder, 72, 102
Internal rotation, 123
Internal rotators, 125
Intervals, 85, 86, 87, 90, 130
  adjusting number of, 94
  longer, 95–96
  shorter, 94–95
  timed, 89
Interval times, 87
  rest and, 92
Intrinsic muscles, strengthening,
  124, 125–26
Inward sweep, 61
Ironman, 3, 54, 59, 77, 130
  collision at, 70
  creatures at, 111
  lessons from, 29
  open water and, 105

Ironman (cont'd)
  preparing for, 14
  shaving for, 132

Kickboards, 101, 101 (fig.)
Kick-on-side (KOS) drills, 34, 39,
    39 (fig.), 51, 76, 114, 115
  with one stroke, 40, 40 (fig.)
  with three strokes, 40
Kicks:
  backstroke, 57, 58 (fig.)
  breaststroke, 61, 62, 62 (fig.), 63
  breathing and, 78
  butterfly, 62, 65 (fig.), 66
  core and, 23
  dolphin, 63
  drills for, 37–40
  efficient, 21, 22, 23, 98
  fins and, 102
  flutter, 23 (fig.), 55, 56
  four-beat, 75, 76
  freestyle, 23, 75
  learning, 101
  patterns for, 75–76
  power of, 23, 61
  pull and, 25
  six-beat, 75, 76
  sprints and, 22
  streamlined, 56
  two-beat, 75, 76
  underwater, 60
KOS. *See* Kick-on-side drills

Lactic acid, 68, 70, 120
  build up of, 71, 93
Ladder, 88, 95–96
Lateral raise, 125
Lat pull-downs, 127
Law of forces, 20
Lawrence, Dietrich, 29, 121
Leg curls, 127
Leg extensions, 127

Legs:
  oxygen/blood for, 75
  sinking, 7
Lifeguards, 106, 109, 110, 111, 115
Lung volume, 16, 17, 18

Main sets, 86, 87, 91, 92
  sample, 94–96
Massages, 120, 132
Mass starts, problems with, 111
Mattes, Aaron, 119, 121, 126
Meditation, 69, 79
Mind-body connection, 79
Min-max drills, 45, 79
Monofins, 29, 64, 77
Muscles
  balancing, 11, 53
  core, 23, 29, 63
  damage to, 92
  intrinsic, 124, 125–26
  isolating, 119
  prime mover, 126
  shortening, 118

Navigation, 105, 108
Neck, neutral, 57
Negative movement, 125
Negative split, 88
Nose clips, 101
Nutrition, 4

Off strokes, 51
  practicing, 53–54, 55, 66
Open turns, 80
Open water
  backstroke and, 53, 55
  breaststroke and, 53, 59
  drafting in, 108
  speed in, 70
  strokes and, 106
  swimming in, 78, 85, 102-3,
    108-11, 114-15

Overextending entry, 51, 51 (fig.)
Overgliding, 45
Overstretching, 119
Oxygen, 17
 debt, 18
 transfer of, 14, 15–16

Pace clocks, 89–90, 89 (fig.)
Pacing, 78, 125
Paddles
 hand, 100, 100 (fig.), 102
 technique and, 102
 wetsuits and, 112
Perceived effort (PE), 92, 93
Performance
 fear and, 8
 improving, 5, 10, 109, 130, 131
Personal record (PR), 45, 46, 79
Personal trainers, 126
Physical therapists, 126
Physics, swimming, 2, 19–25, 21
 (fig.), 28, 54
Physiology, 15, 31, 94
 stretching and, 119
Pilates, 29, 120–21, 128
Pilates, Joseph, 120
Planing off, 30
Posterior handclasp, 123
Posterior raise, 125
Posture, 29
Power, 4, 23, 25, 29, 93, 129–30
 aerobic, 94–95
 effective, 8
 increasing, 19, 20, 28, 54, 72, 73
 maximum, 28, 79
 pulls and, 61, 79
 range and, 124
 rotation and, 59
 undulation and, 66
PR. *See* Personal record
Prime mover muscles, 126
Propulsion, 22, 24, 27, 36

effective, 8
 increasing, 19, 20, 21, 28, 54, 55
 maximum, 61
Pull buoys, 101 (fig.), 102
Pulls, 23, 26 (fig.), 30, 57, 75
 backstroke, 58 (fig.)
 breaststroke, 61, 62, 62 (fig.)
 butterfly, 64, 65 (fig.)
 correcting, 35, 78, 100
 drills for, 24, 36, 41–44
 efficient, 48
 elbow bend and, 55
 enhancing, 114
 finishing, 69
 kicks and, 25
 longer, 8
 pattern for, 72, 73
 power generation with, 61, 79
 rotation and, 58
 short, 7
 shortening, 78–79
 S-pattern of, 73
 straight arm, 31, 51
 underwater, 60
Pull-ups, 127
Push-offs, 25, 27, 27 (fig.), 80–81,
 89
 etiquette and, 90
 good, 76
 poor, 46, 46 (fig.)
 streamlined, 46, 82
Push-ups, 127

Racing, 92
 pool, 83, 85
Range of motion, 23, 127
 power and, 124
Razor clams, 111
Recovery, 2, 4, 25, 48, 56, 57, 64,
 70, 71, 79, 92
 arm, 8, 31
 blood flow and, 120

Recovery (cont'd)
  burnout/illnesses/injuries and,
    131
  overwater, 60
  windmill, 31
Relaxation, 2, 11, 19, 21, 118
  breathing and, 120
  challenges of, 12-14
  focusing on, 68
  learning, 9-10
Release, 25
Repeat times, rest and, 92
Resistance, 7, 126
  arm recovery, 8
  increasing, 125, 127
Resistance cords, 126
Resistance tubing, 126
Rest, 87-88, 89
  effective, 131
  interval (repeat) times and, 92
Reverse sit-ups, 127
Rotation, 20, 22, 22 (fig.), 23, 71,
    79, 97, 101
  breathing and, 21
  drills for, 37-40
  efficient, 21
  fins and, 102
  hampering, 57
  long-axis, 17, 24, 28, 48-49, 49
    (fig.), 55, 56, 57, 64, 69, 72,
    73, 75, 76
  poor, 75
  power for, 59
  proper, 18, 30
  pull and, 58
  strokes and, 68, 107
Rotator cuff, strengthening, 124,
    125-26
Running, 2, 3, 5, 12, 70, 86, 93, 97,
    114, 130, 131

Saltwater, 97
  buoyancy and, 13, 111, 112

Sample week, 96
Sculling, 12-13, 24, 54, 57, 72-73,
    73 (fig.)
  drills with, 73, 75
S-pull pattern and, 72
Sensation, increasing, 132
Sets, 84, 115
  main, 86, 87, 91, 92, 94-96
Shaving, 113, 131-32
Short finish, 48, 48 (fig.)
Shoulder flexibility, exercises for,
    121, 122 (fig.), 123
Shoulder press, 127
Shoulder rotation, 71-72, 71 (fig.)
Shoulders:
  problems with, 72, 102, 121,
    123, 124
  protecting, 79
  strengthening, 126
  stretching, 126
Shoulder shrugs, 71, 72, 125
Shoulder tendinitis, 121
Sidestroke, 53, 59
Sighting, 107 (fig.)
  breathing and, 106
  efficient, 106-7, 108, 115
Single-arm drill, 43, 43 (fig.), 47,
    48, 51, 72, 75
Single-arm fly, 66
Sinking, 14, 112
Skills:
  fear and, 9
  improving, 9, 10, 12
Slapping entry, 51, 51 (fig.)
Slipstream, 23, 30, 36, 76, 98
Snorkels, 29, 99, 99 (fig.)
Speed, 70
  aerobic, 94-95
  easy, 88
  improving, 6, 7, 30, 34, 35, 106
Spine, elongating, 118
Spitz, Mark, 1, 63

Sprints, 77, 83, 88, 103
   all-out, 71
   breathing and, 68
   distance swimming and, 69–71
   half-pool, 71
   kick and, 22
Sprint triathlons, 3
S-pull pattern, 72–73, 74 (fig.), 75
   sculling and, 72
Squats, 127
Static stretching, 120
   and AI compared, 119
Straight long swims, 96
Straight swims, 96
Streamliner hand paddles, 100, 100
   (fig.), 102
Streamlining, 8, 23, 27, 29, 56, 61,
   63, 66, 76, 82
   drag and, 55
   improving, 20, 25, 28
Strength training, 117, 121
   conventional, 124, 127
   flexibility programs and, 120
   forms of, 124–28
   swim-specific, 79, 124–25
Stress, 2, 86
Stretching, 23, 79, 121, 127
   active isolated, 119–20
   breathing and, 120
   static, 119, 120
Stroke rates, 20, 45, 99
   increasing, 17, 48, 69, 70, 71
Strokes, 11, 12, 51
   arm movement and, 75
   balanced, 18, 68
   breathing and, 15, 16, 17, 18, 68,
    69, 106
   delaying, 45
   distance per, 88
   easy, 71
   extension of, 8, 72
   faster, 47

   idiosyncracies in, 106
   improving, 1, 17, 28, 34, 36, 45,
    100
   open water and, 106
   perfect, 1, 5, 28, 31, 33, 45, 79
   rotation and, 68, 107
   shortened, 69, 106
   technique of, 55, 78
   water polo, 106
   wetsuits and, 113.
   See also Off strokes
Superspeed, 93
Sweeps, handling, 110, 110 (fig.)
Swim bench, 126
Swim improvement curve, 10, 10
   (fig.)
Swimmer's metronome, 99, 99 (fig.)
Swimmer's shoulder, 100
Swimming, 7–10
   distance, 21, 24, 69–71, 75
   fitness, 11, 21, 55, 69, 86
   flat, 48, 107
   group, 133
   head-up, 59, 106, 107
   as lifelong support, 4, 118
   long medium-speed, 70
   long slow, 86
   malaligned/disjointed, 29
   physics of, 2, 19–25, 21 (fig.),
    28, 54
   smart, 51
   time for, 2–3, 130
Swimpower 2, 35
Swimsuits, 97, 98, 131

Take-off, 83, 84
Taper, 131–32
Technique, 1, 3, 4, 24, 34, 46, 48,
   107, 130
   breathing and, 14, 79
   drills for, 5, 33, 45, 85, 86, 94,
    129

Technique (cont'd)
  focusing on, 79, 86, 91, 126
  high-level, 2, 67
  improving, xi, 10, 30, 29, 35, 86,
    91, 112, 126, 133
  individualized, 17, 73
  long-distance, 69
  open-water, 102
  paddles and, 102
  pool-related, 76
  poor, 16, 124
  proper, 47, 84, 103
  recommendations on, 2, 133
  rhythm and, 79
  shoulder, 121
  strength training and, 127
  stroke, 17, 19
  wetsuits and, 113
Tempo Trainer, 70, 99, 99 (fig.)
Tendinitis, 100, 121
Tether, 100
THR. See Threshold
Threshold (THR), 93, 94
Time management, 130
Time trialing, 107
Tools, 33, 70, 98
Toxins, removing, 119, 120
Training, 27
  dry-land, 115, 117, 121
  effective, 2, 3, 86, 89, 130
  improving, xi, 1, 84, 91, 130
  managing, 89–90
  specificity, 126, 127
  structure of, 91–96
  swim/bike/run compared,
    130–31

Treading water, 12–14, 13 (fig.), 19
Treadmills, 100
Triceps stretch, 123, 127
Trunk twists, 127
Turnover, 69
Turns, push-off and, 27

Undulation, 59, 63, 64, 76, 77
  breaststroke, 60
  power from, 66

Vertical kicking drill, 37, 37 (fig.),
    45, 76
Video analysis, 35, 45, 46, 47
Visualization, 3, 24, 73, 129–30,
    132
VO$_2$max, 99, 112

Warm-ups, 14, 15, 16, 86, 91, 93,
    101, 115
  blood flow and, 120
Weather conditions, 85, 105,
    109–10
Wetsuits, 102, 112–13, 132
Workouts. See Training

XTERRA World Championships,
    77, 78

Yoga, 29, 69, 79, 118, 119, 130

Zack, Jurgen, 17, 130
Zoomer fins, 36, 66, 98

About the Author

Steve Tarpinian is the president of Total Training, Inc., a fitness consulting company specializing in swim, bike, run, and triathlon workshops. He is a member of the USA Triathlon National Coaching Committee and a certified USAT Level II coach. He has coached several Ironman champions to success through his online service, Total Training University. Tarpinian is the author of *The Essential Swimmer* (1996) and he has also produced *Swim Power* and *Swim Power 2* videos and DVDs. He has contributed to *Men's Health*, *Fitness Swimmer*, *Swim*, *Triathlete*, and *Inside Triathlon*.

The benefits of Yoga go beyond adding a little range of motion to your limbs. The breathing is integrated in a dynamic way with the movement and emotional/spiritual awareness is available to whatever degree you wish to take it to.

 BY STEVE TARPINIAN with Mary Angela Buffo

Available for orders at www.swimpower.com